The Other Side Of The Ditch
A cartoon century in the New Zealand-Australia relationship

The Other Side Of The Ditch

A cartoon century in the New Zealand-Australia relationship

Ian F. Grant

NEW ZEALAND CARTOON ARCHIVE

1901-2001
Centenary of Federation

In association with
TANDEM PRESS

First published by the New Zealand Cartoon Archive,
Alexander Turnbull Library, P O Box 12349,
Wellington, New Zealand, September 2001

© New Zealand Cartoon Archive, 2001

© Ian F. Grant, 2001

All rights reserved. No part of this publication
may be reproduced, stored in a retrieval system,
or transmitted, in any form or by any means,
electronic, mechanical, photocopying or otherwise
without the prior permission of the copyright owners.

ISBN: 0-9582320-0-8
Design: Graham Kerrisk, Printcraft, Masterton
Distribution: Tandem Books, Auckland
Printed by Publishing Press Limited
31 William Pickering Drive, Albany,
Auckland

Cover cartoon: Malcolm Walker from
Erratic Scratchings, 1984

Contents

The Preface   7
"Cartoons are the quick, gut reaction of cartoonists drawing their inspiration from popular sentiment"

The Introduction   9
"Few countries bicker and grizzle about each other more without actually going to war"

The History   14
"Twelve hundred miles of stormy ocean"

The Politics   29
"The Empire was a way for New Zealand to escape the Australian embrace"

The Economics   45
"The Australian coo-ee, the Australian buck-jumping horse, the Australian stock-whip, and wide-awake hat came into New Zealand pastoral life"

The Sport   61
"On the hilly side of the Tasman, a rugby loss is a disaster of major earthquake proportions"

The Culture   76
"What do 'Advance Australia Fair' and 'God Defend New Zealand' say about their respective national psyches?"

The References   92

The Cartoonists   93

The New Zealand Cartoon Archive   95

Index   96

The Acknowledgements

My grateful thanks to my Cartoon Archive colleague Rachel Macfarlane who has helped, prodded and advised at every stage of this book and exhibition project. I would also thank all the Alexander Turnbull Library staff who have helped in many ways.

The NZ Cartoon Archive appreciates the willingness with which the cartoonists whose work appears in this book, or their representatives, have given permission for their cartoons to appear. The same appalies to the publications where the cartoons first appeared and I must particularly record our thanks to the *New Zealand Herald* for the use of cartoons by Sir Gordon Minhinnick and Laurence Clark. The cartoons in the book and exhibition all come from the NZ Cartoon Archive collection.

We would also like to thank Malcolm Walker for the use of the front cover cartoon and Mark Winter (Chicane) for designing the chapter heading symbol.

This book and accompanying exhibition grew out of discussions with the Australian High Commission in Wellington and the opportunity to commemorate the Centenary of Australian Federation in New Zealand in a distinctive manner. The National Council for the Centenary of Federation's sponsorship and other assistance from the High Commission has made the project possible and it has been a particular pleasure working with public affairs manager Paul Irons.

The accompanying cartoon exhibition in the National Library Gallery has involved a very real partnership with National Library exhibition staff.

As always the NZ Cartoon Archive is grateful for the support of our sponsors. They are: Gault Mitchell Lawyers, L. J. Hooker Ltd, Independent Newspapers Ltd, KPMG, Grant Thornton, Newspaper Publishers Assoc., Norske Skog Tasman Ltd, and Wilson & Horton Ltd.

Finally, as always, heartfelt thanks to Diane, who edits what I write, and has been my partner in work and life for 35 happy and fruitful years.

IFG

The Preface

"Cartoons are the quick, gut reaction of cartoonists drawing their inspiration from popular sentiment"

This book is a cartoonists'-eye-view of the relationship between Australia and New Zealand. A collection of editorial cartoons, with their 'unofficial' insights about an event, a period, a trend or attitudes, can often be more rewarding and instructive than the study of official documents. At their best, cartoons snatch and preserve the essence of an historical moment. Cartoons are, in a sense, the pulse on the feelings of the day - the quick, gut reaction of cartoonists drawing their inspiration from popular sentiment. Today, in an increasingly visual society, cartoons can make a point, show up an injustice, underline an absurdity about a policy or a politician in a pithy, pointed, telling way that is more memorable than the earnest leading article or columns of editorial type.

There has been a strong cartooning connection between Australia and New Zealand. In the same way as Australasian cartoonists have flourished in London – they understand the culture, but are outsiders – Kiwi cartoonists have thrived across the Tasman.

The connection stretches a long way back. Nicholas Chevalier, one of the better known mid-nineteenth century landscape painters in New Zealand, is also credited with being Australia's first cartoonist. Most famously, David Low, after working

The Preface

as a precociously young cartoonist in his native New Zealand, launched his international career in 1911 as a 20 year old drawing for the *Bulletin* in Melbourne. A few years later his *Billy Book*, which captured the essence of the five foot nothing, large-nosed and pugnacious PM Billy Hughes, and sold 60,000 copies, was his entree to a glittering Fleet Street career. Aucklander George Finey, one of Australia's highest paid cartoonists in the 1920s, was famous – and increasingly notorious – for his caricatures and pioneering of modern art. And one of Australia's best loved cartoonists between the wars was Tom Glover, who grew up in Wellington and was accorded a state funeral procession when, only 47, he died at his Sydney *Sun* drawing board.

In this collection there are some early cartoons, but most focus on the last quarter century, and most view the relationship from a New Zealand perspective. A number of prominent Australian cartoonists were asked to contribute. They searched their files and found very little. One, who had best remain anonymous, wrote: "I've done a search of my back catalogue and find that I don't have a single cartoon that refers to New Zealand! Not even a lousy pun making fun of your accents." Another responded: "Now that you mention it, I would have to say I've never done a cartoon about New Zealand."

One exception is Alan Moir. He was born and educated in New Zealand but, in 1973, crossed the Tasman to begin what has become an illustrious cartooning career, liberally dotted with plaudits and awards. He has now worked on major newspapers for more than a quarter century and is widely considered a leading Australian cartoonist. But he remains a New Zealander, which explains the frequency of his cartoons on the relationship between the near neighbours.

Ironically, just as this book went to press, the Afghan refugee crisis and Ansett Australia collapse stimulated a sudden, very rare interest in New Zealand among many Australian cartoonists.

It should also be noted that New Zealand cartoonists are not responsible for the convention of identifying their Australian creations with cork-bobbing hats and swarms of bush flies. The Australians did it to themselves, with a tradition of comic farmers and swaggies stretching back to the 1890s.

Ian F. Grant
September 2001

The Introduction

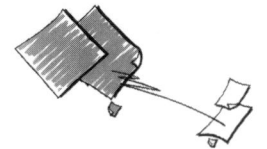

"Few countries bicker and grizzle about each other more without actually going to war"

The Australia-New Zealand relationship is a strange, complex one.

Historically, no two countries on the face of the earth have had more in common – language, Anglo-Saxon heritage, a pioneering push to the edge of the world, white skins on a brown frontier, colonial experience, very similar political and legal systems, fortunes built on pastoral farming, shared trade union traditions, and an obsession with sport. New Zealand and Australia have gone to war together; citizens of each country shuttle back and forth chasing the sun, opportunity or peace and quiet; families make their homes on both sides of the Tasman; the two countries are major trading partners.

Yet few countries bicker and grizzle about each other more without actually going to war.

Well, to be completely honest, New Zealanders do most of the bridling and are quick to take offence whether meant or not. Pulling Aussies down a peg or two ranks highly as a national pastime. Generally, though, New Zealand's air of superiority is a not very convincing cover for a large, collective chip on the shoulder. Or as the Aussies have it: "You can always recognise Kiwis, they're the ones with chips on both shoulders".

New Zealanders might laugh about Australia's

The Introduction

convict past and the average Aussie IQ, but Australians are really far more insulting. They are largely indifferent, with interest in their nearest English-speaking neighbour usually limited to seeing it as a good place for a quiet, quaint and relatively cheap holiday.

The edgy relationship has, of course, been partly determined by size, the scale of things. Australia is huge; New Zealand tiny. The North, South and Stewart Islands, and all the other dots in the ocean New Zealand can make claim to, could be dropped into backblocks New South Wales without unduly scaring the merinos. Australia still digs up amazing wealth; the core of New Zealand's less certain prosperity remains, as it has been for a century and more, the ability to convert grass into tradeable commodities. It has become something of a joke, but not at all untrue, that New Zealanders ask arriving visitors what they think of the country within minutes of their feet touching the tarmac. Australians know they live in a special land – warts and all – and don't much care what anyone else thinks. With five times the population and a more interestingly diverse one, Australia calls itself the 'Lucky Country' and means it; New Zealand has settled, somewhat optimistically, for 'God's Own'.

Camouflaging its inferiority complex in a sort of moral and cultural superiority, New Zealand has tended to exaggerate Australia's convict origins as much as it has romanticised its supposedly more genteel British beginnings. Yet this feeling of being South Seas cousins rather than brothers, together with different political and trading agendas, meant there was surprisingly little interest, on either side of the Tasman, in New Zealand joining the Australian Federation at the beginning of the twentieth century.

In 1901, six British colonies in the South Pacific joined together to create the Australian Federation. The seventh, New Zealand, didn't. There is little evidence, through the subsequent century, that New Zealand has much regretted the decision. It does bear pointing out, though, that it took years of acrimonious wrangling for those six Australian colonies to sort out their differences.

Australia became a federation because there was no way the already well-entrenched states would contemplate any other system. Distance, different economies and population disparities fuelled the suspicion and distrust that led to ill-tempered competition between Sydney and Melbourne. Different gauge railway tracks started and ended at state borders. The rivalry between Australia and New

Zealand may well be excessive, but some of the old prejudices between the Australian states also remain today, State of Origin rugby league matches aside.

For example, a recent re-surveying of a stretch of the boundary between New South Wales and Queensland – ironically for a Centenary of Federation project – showed that NSW's Jennings is now, strictly speaking, in Queensland. Jennings and the twin township of Wallangarra, now technically several hundreds metres deeper into Queensland than previously thought, were an important border crossing point in earlier days. The railway station, with different gauge lines running in and out, and built in two quite distinctive halves, is a considerable architectural curiosity. In 2001, some of Jennings' residents are strongly objecting to the possibility of having to drink in a Queensland pub.

It should also be pointed out that there were periods earlier in the trans-Tasman relationship when Australia was anything but indifferent to what was happening in New Zealand. Between 1861-63, nearly 65,000 fortune-seekers from Australia crowded into South Island ports en route to the new goldfields. There was a time, particularly in the 1890s, when New Zealand's relative prosperity and raft of progressive legislation was much discussed, debated and even admired in Australia. New Zealand smugness grew in direct proportion. By 1901, for one Australian commentator at least, enough was enough. "The name of New Zealand is becoming nauseating; I am sick of its being quoted," he said. In general, Australia and Australians have subsequently taken his point to heart.

This infuriating indifference is at least part of the reason why it is so vitally important for New Zealanders to beat Australians as often as possible. Rugby, netball, cricket or boardroom victories are most satisfying, but almost anything will do. It is puzzling, particularly to the rest of the world, that a victory over the Aussies at rugby is an excuse for national celebration and a loss casts a palpable pall over the country. Political commentators factor Bledisloe Cup results into election year calculations.

The wisdom of more closely integrating the two economies is rarely questioned today. At a recent conference in Auckland former Australian Prime Minister Paul Keating promoted the "two countries, one system" approach. While rejecting closer political ties, he said economic union with Australia, five times its size, would be more important to New Zealand than bi-lateral free trade agreements with countries in Asia or the Americas. But he was far

The Introduction

from certain that it would happen. "Australia has always been accommodating about the prospect of economic union with New Zealand," he said, "but there are many parts of the New Zealand psyche that find it difficult to deal with Australia."

Others, like Australian writer Thomas Keneally, see an inevitability about closer political ties following economic integration, but gradually over time. "In this debate New Zealand's always been cast as a maiden, but that's never washed with me because I've seen the All Blacks in full cry. Australia has always been cast as a great hairy, boozy, ugly, loud suitor who may, given half a chance, have his way with her no matter what she says. I don't think there's that much passion and desire. I think it's a very cool, surreptitiously holding hands and walking into the future sort of thing."

Whatever the heart might say, the head is certainly capable of calculating the advantage of political integration. In 1901, had New Zealand joined the Federation, it would have ranked third in wealth and population behind New South Wales and Victoria; in 2001, despite its tumble down OECD performance ladder, New Zealand would still rank fourth in seniority. And the immediate advantages are obvious: a faster growth of per capita income, a much larger, more diversified economy for companies, a more stable currency.

Cartoon by Tom Scott.

Not that all the advantages would flow in one direction; there's no other way Australia could acquire, in one king hit, nearly four million English-speaking immigrants and a 12 percent fillip to the GNP. And, as Australian political scientist Bob Catley has noted: "Australia would get some proper mountains and New Zealand a barrier reef."

Nevertheless, while there is an inexorable trend towards economic union – pushed along by the forces of globalisation – closer political ties seem as unlikely today as they did in 1901. Politically, the two countries are drifting further apart – despite geological evidence that has them inching together again. Optimistically, Australia looks north for trade, more apprehensively in defence terms. New Zealand anticipates a benign Polynesian future. New Zealand is less able, or even willing, to be weaned away from its largely Anglo-Saxon traditions. Australia has had a large injection of south European and Asian blood. As Australian jurist Justice Kirby said: "The 'crimson thread of kinship', which Sir Henry Parkes said linked Australians and New Zealanders is now looking thin and frayed."

The Centenary of Federation has provided an opportunity for the two countries to restore, at least symbolically, something of those old, special bonds of kinship. In April this year prime ministers John Howard and Helen Clark dedicated New Zealand's centenary year gift to Australia – bronze arches that span the entrance of Anzac Parade in Canberra. The design, representing the handles of a basket or kete, is based on the traditional Maori proverb that, loosely translated, says: "You at that, and me at this, handle of the basket", and is a metaphor for New Zealand and Australia's shared experiences in many spheres during the last century.

Ultimately, of course, substance carries more weight than symbolism. New Zealand political commentator Colin James recently wrote: "To Australians the 'nz' in 'Anzac' is a consonantal hiccup in a name to which they claim proprietory rights. We count in Canberra and the state capitals not as an opportunity but as, at best, a requisite afterthought and, more often, a niggling nuisance."

The fact that the provision to join the Federation is still in the Australian Constitution is not because of any hope, or particular wish, that New Zealand will. It's simply that the Australian lawmakers have forgotten to take it out.

The History

"Twelve hundred miles of stormy ocean"

It should not really have been such a strange idea for New Zealand to become part of Australia in 1901 – it already had been just that early in the century before. Or more accurately, a very mixed collection of British subjects in New Zealand, flotsam and jetsam washing up on a convenient shore, missionaries and hard-eyed sealers, whalers and flax traders, were somewhat ambiguously under the jurisdiction of the colony of New South Wales from about 1813 onwards. More formally, for a few months following annexation by Great Britain in 1840, New Zealand was, to no-one's satisfaction, a 'dependency' of New South Wales.

In the early years of the nineteenth century there was substantial trans-Tasman trade, at which Maori excelled. In the late 1830s, with plans underway in London to establish New Zealand settlements and grudging acceptance by the British government that it would have to administer them more systematically, some of Australia's newly-rich land speculators attempted, unsuccessfully as it turned out, to grab large chunks of New Zealand in advance of the first settlers.

In the decades following 1840, trade and the movement of people between the Antipodean colonies ebbed and flowed depending on the state of their separate economies.

The gold rushes and land wars of the 1860s brought

The History

"UNION IS STRENGTH."
A LESSON BETTER LEARNT LATE THAN NEVER.

This was possibly the first cartoon on the subject of federation.
At a time when Victoria was combating recession with a wall of tariff protection, Gavan Duffy, one of the state's radical politicians, was promoting political union for the seven Australasian colonies. The venerable English *Punch* magazine had a number of copyright-ignoring imitators in Australia and New Zealand.

Union Is Strength: A Lesson Better Learnt Late Than Never, Anonymous, *Melbourne Punch,* 26 January 1860.

The History

significant numbers of Australians to the South and North Islands respectively.

New Zealand governments, central and provincial, watched events in Australia closely enough to avoid the mistakes that led to rebellion and tragedy on the Victorian goldfields. The thousands of miners who poured into the country, mainly from the Australian diggings, were given more rights than previously and Vincent Pyke, a highly effective Australian miners' advocate, was put in charge of the Otago goldfields. New Zealand observed the unbridled power of squatters in New South Wales and Victoria and punitive industrial legislation in the Australian colonies – and introduced policies that broke up the great estates and gave more protection to the working man.

In 1863-4, the New Zealand government recruited nearly 2500 military settlers from New South Wales, Victoria and Tasmania, promising them grants of confiscated Maori land at the end of hostilities. They stiffened the ranks and resolve of the New Zealand Militia, but later found it hard to prosper in the poorly planned military settlements.

Undeniably, New Zealand and the Australian colonies had a great deal in common. They shared a language, and accents still indistinguishable to most other people, an Anglo-Saxon kinship, the same colonial relationship within the British Empire, and institutions with a common history. Relative proximity at the bottom of the world was reason enough for self-interested trade and cultural co-operation. Yet, from early on, there seemed an obsessive wish to identify, prod, even exaggerate the differences.

In New Zealand at least, there was a preoccupation with Australia's penal settlement beginnings. Perhaps this, and New Zealand's more orderly development, together with very different landscapes in terms of size, climate, flora and fauna, helped embellish the larrikin Aussie and more prim, stolid Kiwi stereotypes. Certainly, increasingly well-honed competitive instincts and diverging views on a number of issues, best explain why a lengthy parade of conferences, conventions and meetings among Australasian politicians in the 1860s and 1870s achieved comparatively little.

Understandably, communications and trade were of prime importance in the mid-nineteenth century. Ocean mail services that carried everything from dispatches to and from the Colonial Office to the books and periodicals providing the psychologically important, if tenuous, cultural links, were crucial. The unsatisfactory P & O service – via Cairo, overland to Suez, on to Ceylon, then across the Indian Ocean and around the south of Australia – pleased no-one, but it remained

The History

A COOL IDEA.

Hollo! Bob—What going to spend the Winter on an Iceberg?

Bob.—Well, not exactly, but I'm off to Dunedin, and that's much the same thing.

Between 1861-63, many thousands of fortune-seekers from Australia crowded into South Island ports, principally Port Chalmers, en route to the new Otago goldfields. A particularly harsh winter in 1862, with snow on the ground for six weeks, sent some Victorian miners packing, but news of more finds encouraged others to try their luck.

A Cool Idea, Anonymous, *Melbourne Punch*, 5 March 1863.

The History

because there was no agreement on an alternative. Attempts to establish mail services via Panama, Singapore and San Francisco all had their difficulties, usually because the colonial administrations, in varying combinations, could not agree.

There was less acrimony over electric telegraph communication, which became a reality for the South Seas colonies when the cable from Europe reached Bombay in 1870. Nevertheless, a scheme for New South Wales and Queensland, supported by New Zealand, to link to Bombay via a cable from Queensland to Java and Singapore was comprehensively upstaged by South Australia's land cable to Darwin. In 1872 this was successfully hooked up to a cable from Singapore and ushered in a revolutionary new communications era.

Trade was no simple matter either. The Australasian colonies were not free to make their own rules. The idea of inter-colonial preferential trading was anathema to the British government which, in the 1870s, was a passionate advocate of international free trade. Eventually, the colonies won their trade concessions but, perversely, there was little change to trans-Tasman trading patterns. New Zealand trade, very largely imports, was almost exclusively with Victoria and New South Wales. And the negotiation of preferential treatment was of little value, or interest, as nearly all New Zealand exports went to Britain.

In October 1871, *The Melbourne Age* summed up meetings between New Zealand and Australian colonial politicians, succinctly and with perception: "These Conferences are doubly abortive. On the principal questions no decision is arrived at, and on the smaller ones the resolutions are never acted on." Even then it was clear that there was a gulf, as wide as the Tasman, in the perceptions and expectations of New Zealand and Australian politicians.

There was, of course, some constructive co-operation, but mainly among officials, particularly the respective Agents-General in London who could talk quietly about financial and South Pacific defence matters, with Whitehall and the Houses of Parliament no more than a saunter away.

One area of developing common interest – although even here there were different agendas – was the future of the South Pacific region as the United States, France, Germany and Russia all flexed their imperial muscles. At inter-colonial conferences in 1880-1 and 1883, there were more urgent attempts to persuade Britain to safeguard its Pacific dominance – and a growing sense of the security blanket attraction of joining together in a federation of colonies.

Yet as federation began to be talked about with more

The History

A DASTARDLY ATTEMPT

VICTORIA.– "Let's see if this will upset their improved credit and prosperity, confound them."
N.Z. Opposition Press. – "Go it my boy, I've tried to do it myself many a time, but hadn't the strength."

By the mid-1890s New Zealand's economy was picking up strongly to the discomfort of both the opposition press at home and politicians in Victoria, who were staunch supporters of federation. The latter feared that New Zealand's growing prosperity and independence might slow progress towards federation.

A Dastardly Attempt,
Ashley Hunter,
New Zealand Graphic,
25 May 1895.

The History

urgency, the differences between the Australian colonies and New Zealand appeared in starker relief to politicians who were not about to have their ambitions swamped in a much larger political entity. While it was too early to identify anything as concrete as national identity there was a developing 'separateness' felt in New Zealand. After all, as early as 1857, Governor Sir Thomas Gore-Browne had reported to the Colonial Office that a "separate and independent power and destiny is fitting for this Colony".

So there is little evidence that the New Zealand people, press or politicians were ever seriously interested in joining in political union with the Australian colonies. For years, at the meetings and conferences New Zealand politicians attended, federation was little more than an academic talking point. When the Australian colonies finally found the political will to hold their rivalries and ambitions in check, New Zealand was forced to make some response. It is significant that there was so little debate about what that response should be.

Following the 1883 inter-colonial conference in Sydney, which put a little more flesh on the Federal Council concept first raised two years before, there was some muted and confused discussion of the issue in New Zealand, particularly during the 1884 election campaign. It quickly dropped off everyone's political agenda.

The speech by New Zealand's representative, Sir John Hall, at the 1890 Melbourne conference was stirring stuff. His "Nature has made twelve hundred impediments to the inclusion of New Zealand in any such federation in the twelve hundred miles of stormy ocean" was much quoted and never thought too much about. No one pointed out that it was a lame excuse indeed – there was almost twice the distance, and much of it distinctly inhospitable, between Perth and Sydney, and many US states were much further away from Washington and each other without serious impediment to that nation's federal system.

At the same conference Sir Henry Parkes, Premier of New South Wales, made his famous toast to a united Australia: "The crimson thread of kinship runs through us all".

In 1891, it is unlikely that many would have disagreed when Premier John Ballance spoke against a federation involving New Zealand: "We might supply Australia with a few oats, but we should lose our freedom". Later in the decade, Prime Minister Richard J. Seddon, whose larger-than-life politicking was well known on both sides of the Tasman, was more interested in New Zealand leading a Pacific Islands grouping than being submerged in a greater Australia. In fact, New

The History

"THE MAN IN POSSESSION."

" I say, mate, 'ere come some more o' them bloomin' unemployed!"
"Well, spread yerself out, and tell 'em there aint no more room for nobody!"

The Australian maritime strike of 1890 spread across the Tasman when a New Zealand ship in Sydney was worked by non-union labour. New Zealand's Maritime Council, affiliated to its Australian counterpart, had little option but to call out its men. The first real flexing of union muscles in either country collapsed quickly as rural workers and unpaid 'volunteers' replaced striking seamen and wharf labourers. Subsequently, there was little co-operation between union movements. In fact, unionists were vocal in their disapproval of the rising number of unemployed Australian workers coming to New Zealand.

"The Man In Possession",
Ashley Hunter,
New Zealand Graphic,
10 February 1894.

The History

Zealand had no representatives at the conventions that finally hammered out a draft federation constitution and this, although it made provision for a seventh colony to be included, was never debated by the politicians in Wellington.

In June 1899 when New South Wales decided, after much procrastination, to join in, federation was suddenly a reality. But the New Zealand response was predictably muted. An Auckland public meeting formed the Australasian Federation League, which failed to generate much interest or branches elsewhere. In 1900, Prime Minister Seddon set up a Royal Commission on Federation, effectively after the event, in part to check out his political instincts about the issue. His government was also cautious enough to ask the Colonial Office to amend the Commonwealth Bill so that New Zealand could join the federation at a later date on the original terms. Collectively, the Australian colonies were not amused.

Submissions to the Royal Commission were predictable. Manufacturers and trade unionists, both concerned about competition, were strongly opposed. Only farmers, fearing tariffs and sensing opportunities, were mildly enthusiastic. Overall, two-thirds of submissions were against federation. There was a strong whiff of moral superiority in the air as well as a genuine, if not always well reasoned, belief that New Zealand society – with its pioneering welfare legislation, egalitarianism and lack of monopolies, and comparatively enlightened treatment of Maori – risked too much if it became part of Australia.

Also, New Zealand's primary allegiance had always been – and remained – to Britain, for emotional and very practical reasons. Acclimatization societies were committed to turning New Zealand, as much as terrain and climate allowed, into a sort of Britain of the southern seas; Australia, with its much higher percentage of Irish and many of its earliest arrivals shipped out courtesy of His Majesty's justice system, had less affection for the 'Old Country'. New Zealand's economic ties to Britain were also strong. Particularly since the beginnings of refrigerated shipping in the early 1880s, New Zealand's exports had gone almost exclusively to Britain. On the other hand, the Australian colonies had a much higher dependence on trade amongst themselves.

William Pember Reeves, man on the spot and one of New Zealand's most perceptive observers, accurately summed up the situation in 1902: "New Zealanders never seriously contemplated coming in; nor have the Australians supposed that they would, or expended much time or trouble in efforts to enlist them."

The History

"AUT CAESAR AUT NULLUS"
CHORUS OF FEDERALISTS: "Don't you want to come aboard of our ship?"
Hon. R. S. ...: "What? Give up my position as skipper of this 'ere little craft to be a bo'sun's mate along of you? No thanks." (Proceeds to paddle his own little canoe.)

A draft federal constitution drawn up in 1891 for the discussion and approval of colonial governments was not even tabled in the New Zealand Parliament and there were no representatives at the final, bargaining conferences in the late 1890s.
New Zealand Prime Minister Richard John Seddon, a popular figure on both sides of the Tasman, had little enthusiasm for weakening New Zealand's sovereignty, his political power, or his imperial ambitions for the South Pacific.

"Aut Caesar Aut Nullus", Ashley Hunter, *New Zealand Graphic,* 8 July 1899.

The History

New Zealand supporters of federation stressed the shared British stock, language, Queen, God, and trade possibilities. New Zealand would progress by 'leaps and bounds', with an assured market for cereals, fruit and some manufactured goods. South Seas isolation was another reason for embracing federation. There was uneasiness about growing German power and French intentions in the Pacific; there was also fear, however irrational, of the 'yellow peril'.

Federation In The Air, Ashley Hunter, *New Zealand Graphic,* 16 September 1899.

FEDERATION IN THE AIR.
ONE POSSIBLE VIEW OF THE POSITION OF NEW ZEALAND.

The History

THE UNGRATEFUL BEGGAR.
EX-PREMIER REID (interviewed after touring New Zealand): In my opinion, no sort of bad legislation can keep New Zealand back.
PREMIER DICK (across the water): Who says bad legislation? And this is gratitude! After my free railway passes, my special brand of Wanganui champagne, and the fat cigars I gave him, too.

Sir George Reid, a late enthusiast for federation, was New South Wales Premier from 1897-99 and Australian Prime Minister in 1904-05. He visited New Zealand while out of office, early in 1900; like many Australian politicians at the time he was impressed with the relative prosperity and apprehensive about the Liberals' radical legislative programme.

"The Ungrateful Beggar",
William Blomfield,
N.Z. Observer and Free Lance,
10 February 1900.

25

The History

Very much at the last minute, the New Zealand government asked for three amendments to the Commonwealth Bill – involving legal and defence matters and seeking the right to join the Commonwealth for another seven years on the same terms as the original states. William Pember Reeves, New Zealand's Agent-General in London, annoyed the Australian colonies with his reported remarks that a further referendum might be needed. The Australians had held nine referenda in the previous two years and there was no intention of holding any more, particularly as the decision to proceed had been a close run thing in New South Wales.

The Agent-General Putting his Foot in it, Ashley Hunter, *New Zealand Graphic,* 7 April 1900.

The Agent-General Putting his Foot in it.

The History

HOW WE SEE IT

THE OGRE: "Come into these arms." NEW ZEALAND: "Nay, sir, those arms bear chains."

In 1900, a Royal Commission heard submissions throughout New Zealand and the overwhelming conclusion was that local interests would be swamped by Australia's size, population and resources. While notions about nationhood were rarely if ever articulated there was still a strong sense that joining the Federation would swamp a growing sense of a separate identity. Certainly New Zealanders had grown accustomed to thinking of themselves as different from Australians, an idea first fostered in New Zealand Company publicity from the late 1830s.

How We See It, Scatz, *New Zealand Graphic,* 20 October 1900.

The History

New Zealand felt sufficiently distinctive and apart from the other Australasian colonies to give surprisingly little thought to joining with the six others in 1901. Gallipoli is widely credited for the first stirrings of New Zealand nationalism, but there are clear indications that, however unformed and unspoken they may have been, they were there by the turn of the century.

"As long as New Zealanders look back ...",
Tom Scott,
The Paua and the Glory,
1982.

Gallipoli...

"As long as New Zealanders look back lads they will surely concur that nationhood was forged right here on this anvil!!"

"How come there is never a Turkish sniper when you need one?"

The Politics

"The Empire was a way for New Zealand to escape the Australian embrace"

New Zealand historian F. L. W. Wood has written: "When in 1900 businessmen and politicians talked of the differences in character between the two countries this was nine-tenths of it nonsense. Within ten or twenty years it had grown up into a significant reality."

It is no coincidence that at the same time the Federation issue was being resolved, New Zealand's enthusiastic despatch of soldiers to the Anglo-Boer War, rebuffing suggestions of a combined Australasian contingent, was heightening a nationalistic consciousness.

As diplomat Denis McLean has put it: "Content to focus on its own links with London, New Zealand largely lost interest in dealings across the Tasman. The feeling was mutual. The Empire was a way for New Zealand to escape the Australian embrace." With the Federation issue out of the way, political contact across the Tasman was mainly concerned with co-operation, or lack of it, over defence and economic matters. It should not be forgotten, however, that Australia exported to New Zealand a parade of union activists who were to become major political figures.

By the closing decades of the nineteenth century, niggling concerns on both sides of the Tasman about

The Politics

Britain's once omnipotent naval power led to the colonies contributing to the cost of beefing up the Royal Navy's Australian Squadron. Following Federation, the new Commonwealth of Australia's attention shifted to a navy of its own, leaving New Zealand apprehensive about anything that might compromise the Royal Navy's protective shield. Prime Minister Joseph Ward's flamboyant response to the Australian decision in 1908 to build three destroyers was to offer Britain a battleship, the excuse being a perceived acceleration in Germany's naval build-up. Australia, not amused, grudgingly followed suit. An early act of New Zealand's Reform government, in power in 1912, was to acquire a training cruiser; it was the first hesitant step towards a separate naval force.

With Europe's gathering war clouds obvious even in the South Pacific, there was more incentive for the two governments to co-operate with training and personnel exchanges. As well, both countries had accepted the concept of expeditionary forces, or 'forward defence' in today's parlance. The culmination of these closer links came early in the First World War when 38 troopships of New Zealanders and Australians sailed across the Indian Ocean to Egypt, under the watchful eye of the Australian navy. There, New Zealanders and Australians formed the Australian and New Zealand Army Corps (ANZAC) which fought with bloody, futile distinction at Gallipoli. At the same time, Gallipoli was an important milestone in both countries' growing belief in themselves as distinct, separate nations.

In the 1920s Australia was committed to building up its own navy; New Zealand's embryonic fleet was simply a 'division' of the Royal Navy. When Britain asked for help to build the Singapore Naval Base, New Zealand paid more than it could sensibly afford. Australia paid nothing, but further strengthened its own navy. Trans-Tasman co-operation was almost at a standstill when New Zealand decided not to send army officer cadets to Duntroon Military College for a number of years.

Although there were some attempts to mend the defence relationship late in the 1930s, the gulf was not easily bridged, even though Hitler's Germany looked increasingly ominous. Labour, in power for the first time in New Zealand, had always been sceptical of the Singapore strategy and was more in favour of a regional approach than its predecessor governments. But before much critical co-ordination could be achieved, Britain and its Empire were at

The Politics

IT MUST BE A BUG

The Australian and New Zealand governments were diametrically opposed politically for only three or four years out of the four decades from the early 1940s. Labour was in power in New Zealand from 1935-49 and in Australia from 1941-49; Clement Atlee's Labour Party won office in Britain at the end of the Second World War, remaining in government until 1951.

It Must Be A Bug, Gordon Minhinnick, *New Zealand Herald*, 23 February 1950.

The Politics

war again. In an eerie repetition of history, the first echelons of troops from Australia and New Zealand sailed together again to Egypt. But there the similarities ended. The ANZAC spirit was not rekindled on the battlefield and, after the fall of Singapore in 1942, the Australian government ordered its troops back to the Pacific while most of the New Zealand military effort remained in the Middle East and then Europe.

During the 1940s Labour governments in both countries shared similar national and international ideals. The ANZAC Pact (more commonly called the Canberra Pact in New Zealand), signed in 1944, underscored their determination to play an assertive part in the international organisations that would attempt to shape the course of post-war events. Australian and New Zealand political leaders were vocal at the San Francisco conference that established the United Nations, and both countries played prominent roles in the beginnings of the Food and Agriculture Organisation (FAO) and World Health Organisation (WHO), which mirrored their social-democratic ideals. They were less enthusiastic, in a world suddenly littered with acronyms, about the International Monetary Fund (IMF); for Labour governments it raised the spectre of unscrupulous international bankers.

To anxious Antipodean governments, the chain of events following the 1949 victory of the communists in China seemed, at the time, ample evidence of the validity of President Eisenhower's 'domino' theory. It strongly influenced the signing, in 1951, of the ANZUS Treaty, an agreement that ensured close military links between the United States, Australia and New Zealand for the next 34 years. The Korean War, Malayan 'Emergency', Indonesian 'Confrontation' and the first tentative United States' decisions that led, step by step, to the disastrous Vietnam War, all seemed to point to the inexorable spread of communism.

There were subtle differences in the Australian and New Zealand approaches to some of these crises. For example, history and proximity meant that Australia was more muted in its response to Sukarno's 'Confrontation' than New Zealand. But there was solid agreement, particularly after British bungling and weakness were exposed during the 'Suez Affair' in 1956, that New Zealand and Australia's concerns should be focussed in the Southeast Asia-Pacific regions and that the United States was their most reliable ally. Loyalty might have been transferred, but the same largely unquestioning acceptance saw

The Politics

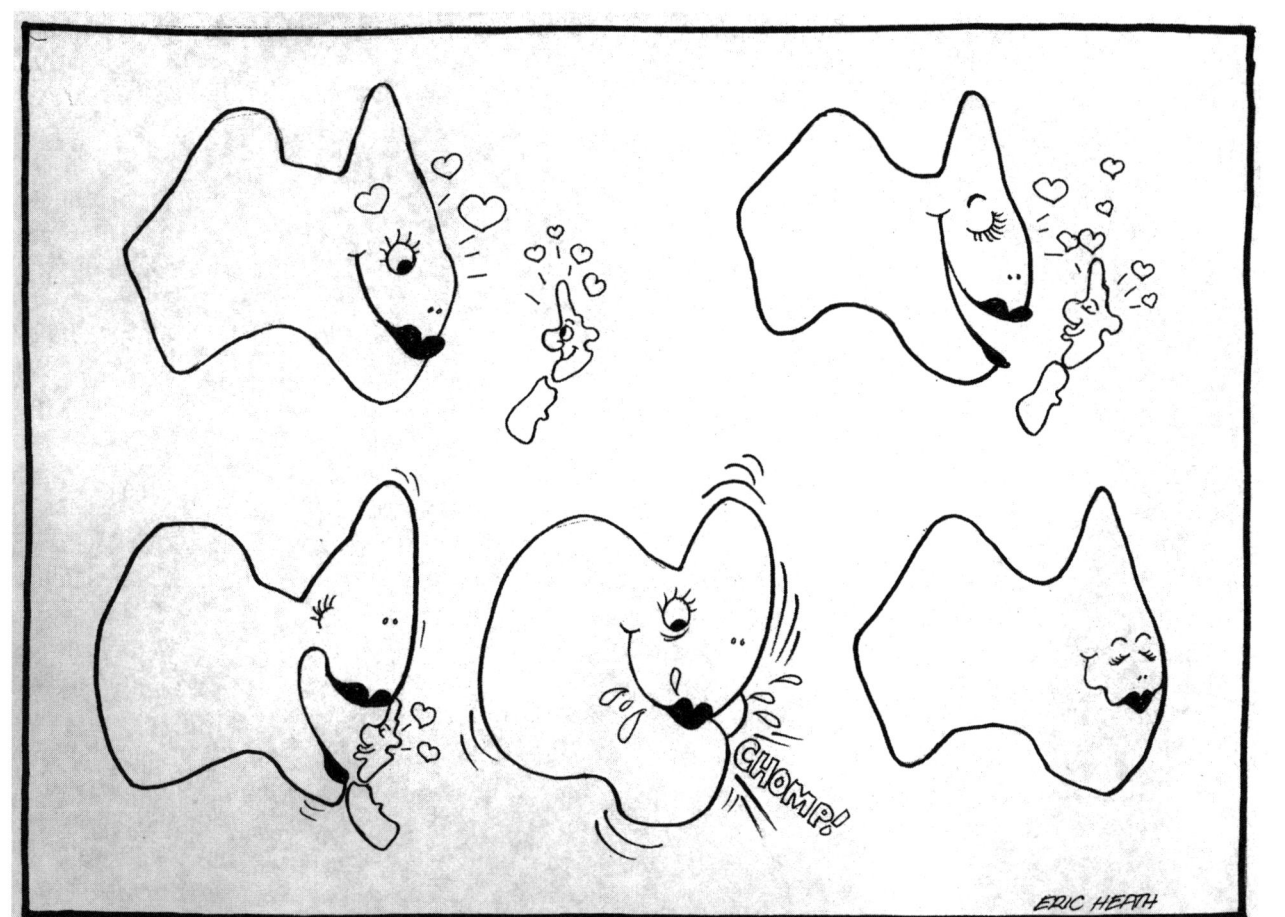

At times there have been flurries of interest in the idea of trans-Tasman political union. One occasion was during the Commonwealth leaders conference in Zambia in 1979. While dismissing speculation of a falling out with his Australian counterpart, Malcolm Fraser, Prime Minister Muldoon gave a typically cautious nod in the direction of closer economic – but not political – integration. *The Dominion* editorialised: "When Australians proclaim they want to save us, we had better be on our guard. They are cunning rascals whose practice suits their purse and their sharp opinion of themselves."

"Chomp", Eric Heath, *The Dominion*, 17 August 1979

The Politics

Australia and New Zealand follow the United States into the Vietnam quagmire.

After the United States' ignominious retreat from Vietnam it became fashionable to admit, as academics had long known, that the engulfing tentacles of 'international communism' had more to do with propaganda than reality. China and the USSR were distinctively separate countries quite capable of flexing massive nationalistic muscles, and in the 1970s and 1980s the United States, and its allies, reached trade-focused accommodations with them both. In doing so, the perceived and real security concerns in the South Pacific lessened.

Of greater real threat to New Zealand and Australia, or at least to their standards of living, had been Britain's stubborn determination to join the EEC, which finally succeeded at the third attempt in 1971. It was a further weakening in the relationship with Britain, particularly for Australia, which had already developed healthy trading relationships with a number of other countries. New Zealand, because it had the most to lose under Europe's Common Agricultural Policy, and said so eloquently, was granted more generous UK trade concessions.

Trade between Australia and New Zealand had been practically moribund until the 1960s when politicians eventually confronted the blindingly obvious: a trans-Tasman free-trading relationship would make a great deal of political and economic sense. As economic co-operation has developed, NAFTA maturing into CER, talk of merged stock exchanges and a single currency led to speculation about going the whole political hog. But Canterbury University economist Wolfgang Rosenberg was wrong when he wrote that CER would "lead to the practical end of New Zealand's short history as a nation state".

While the two countries have moved about as close to economic integration as is possible without formal economic union, key foreign policy and defence differences could not be much more sharply defined. There has been constructive co-operation in the South Pacific, working together, for example, to form the South Pacific Forum that has helped ensure the survival of a number of tiny, newly independent Pacific Island states. But Australia is a wealthy, middle-level power, close to Asia, with thousands of miles of coastline and an empty interior and this adds up to a bi-partisan 'self reliance-self-defence' policy, with a close, non-negotiable relationship with the United States. New Zealand, on the other hand, sees itself as a small, isolated nation

The Politics

AN OFFER YOU CAN'T REFUSE

It was undoubtedly naïve of David Lange and his government to think that the declaration of a New Zealand nuclear-free zone would be tolerated by its ANZUS allies. The United States refused to confirm or deny whether visiting warships were nuclear armed or powered, effectively bringing the tripartite defence treaty to an abrupt end. The result, despite pressure from Australian Prime Minister Bob Hawke, was an uneasy truce.

An Offer You Can't Refuse,
Trace Hodgson,
N.Z. Listener,
1 September 1984.

with a South Pacific perspective, aware that what international clout it can muster will come from a 'good global citizen' role rather than any puny military posturing.

The most serious fracture in the trans-Tasman relationship developed when the Labour government, elected in New Zealand in 1984, put principle before pragmatism and declared the country a nuclear-free zone – and that included port visits by nuclear armed or powered United States' ships. Ingenuously, PM David Lange claimed this did not affect the ANZUS Treaty; the United States, refusing to disclose sensitive information about its warships, brought the tripartite agreement to an abrupt end. Australia placed no such conditions on US warship visits, and continued separate military exercises with the other two countries.

At the beginning of the 1980s both Australia and New Zealand had highly regulated and subsidised economies and shared poor growth, high unemployment and inflation. Their responses to these problems were similar; the outcomes were markedly different – with Australia much more successful – largely because of two significantly different political systems. In New Zealand it was possible for the New-Right zealots, principally Labour's Roger Douglas and National's Ruth Richardson, to ram through the House of Representatives, with minimal debate and limited popular support, economic liberalisation policies that at times owed more to ideology than practical common sense. Australian politicians of the time had much the same impulses, but State legislatures and two Houses of Parliament in Canberra filtered out the more extreme and unworkable measures and slowed down the process.

As a consequence, economic growth during the 1990s was far stronger and more sustained in Australia and there was a widening gap between the average income there and in New Zealand. This put some strain on what is surely the most enduring, and impressive, aspect of the trans-Tasman relationship, the free, two-way movement of citizens to live and work in either country. During the 70 years this right has been specifically legislated for, the migratory flows have swung back and forth, but recently most of it has been into Australia, fuelled by the triple attraction of lower taxes, higher wages and greater opportunity.

New Zealand trade minister Jim Sutton has said that political union between the two countries would produce "much discontent for debatable gains". And it is New Zealand which would, in theory at least, gain the most. Some pundits say there is already a

The Politics

New Zealand's membership of the ANZUS alliance was problematical from the moment David Lange announced, as an adjunct to the country's newly minted nuclear-free stance, that this explicitly included port visits by nuclear armed or powered ships from any nation.
To provide such confirmation, the United States argued, would compromise a key element of their global defence strategy.

ANZUS,
Peter Bromhead,
Auckland Star,
27 September 1984.

The Politics

remarkable amount of political contact; certainly it would be difficult to find anywhere two other sovereign countries whose politicians and bureaucrats meet, confer and conference so regularly. Others chip in with the thought that, in practical terms, New Zealand and, to a lesser extent, Australia have already lost their economic sovereignty in this age of globalisation.

Yet nationalism, on both sides of the Tasman, is obviously not snuffed out by increasing economic integration. There is now a long history of difference, real or imagined. New Zealand is increasingly peripheral to Australia's vision. There is now concern in Canberra about a seeming economic liberalism backslide in New Zealand and a willingness to let the state sector grow again. At the same time, there is no other way Australia could instantly add GNP of Queensland proportions to the national economy. The fear in Wellington, though, is that a new, seventh state would be seen by Australians as another Tasmania.

And those who ask, rarely facetiously, what would happen to the All Blacks, do have a point. If branding is the key to success in the global marketplace, the island nation of New Zealand may continue to have more appeal in cheese and lamb marketing terms and more allure for the tourists who are likely to outnumber the locals in the South Island before the century is much older. It is also reassuring to think that New Zealand's 'good global citizen' brand will be continuing, for the foreseeable future and possibly beyond, to cast its vote on the side of the angels around all those international conference tables.

In September 2001 trans-Tasman relations were suddenly at their lowest ebb for some years. Many New Zealanders were perplexed by Canberra's attitude towards a boatload of Afghan refugees trapped in diplomatic limbo in the Indian Ocean near Australia's remote Christmas Island outpost. Then Australian unions and media gave more attention to New Zealand than usual, to vent their anger at the collapse of Ansett Australia, blaming owners Air New Zealand, and the New Zealand government, and threatening boycotts of anything with a New Zealand label. There was more than a little irony in the union protest banner messages 'Can't play rugby [following another Bledisloe Cup loss]. Can't run an airline'. Air New Zealand's pursuit of an already troubled Ansett resulted directly from the Australian government's 1994 decision to abort an earlier memorandum of understanding for a single trans-Tasman aviation market.

The Politics

Eric Heath used a number of variations of this effective visual symbol for the breakup of ANZUS. The visit of the *USS Truxton* to Wellington in 1982, and the United States' government's refusal to discuss its weaponry, helped firm up Labour's determination to declare New Zealand nuclear-free and to ban port visits by nuclear armed or powered naval vessels.

A....US, Eric Heath, *The Dominion,* 5 February 1985.

The Politics

The fourth Labour government in New Zealand, headed by David Lange, followed wildly contradictory policies: a rigidly right wing economic agenda and a radically independent foreign policy, its centrepiece the determination to declare the country nuclear-free and oppose nuclear armaments globally.

"Cowboys", Bob Brockie, *National Business Review*, 15 August 1986.

The Politics

With the ANZUS Treaty effectively dead, New Zealand, needing to shore up its rocky bilateral relationship with Australia, signed up, in November 1989, to the ANZAC Ship Project. Critics saw more than a little arm twisting on the part of Australian defence minister Kim Beazley when it was announced that New Zealand would acquire two new frigates, with options on two more, at a cost of $2 billion.

The Arms Talks,
Chicane,
PSA Journal,
Feb-March 1989.

The Politics

Paul Keating's outspokenness did not noticeably diminish during the Australian Prime Minister's visit to New Zealand in 1993. There was not a close relationship between Keating's Labour government and Jim Bolger's National one, and the Australians were impatient of what they perceived as New Zealand's dithering on defence and economic matters. It was Keating who, in October 1994, aborted the memorandum of understanding, signed two years before, to create a single trans-Tasman aviation market.

"I want to assure the citizens …",
Tom Scott,
Evening Post,
21 May 1993.

42

The Politics

THE SPIRIT OF ANZAC

In 2001, Australian and New Zealand defence priorities and spending diverged more sharply than previously. While John Howard's Australian government boosted defence expenditure and re-equipped strike elements in its airforce, Helen Clark's New Zealand government abandoned all pretence that the RNZAF was capable of a military role and concentrated on better equipping the army to play a peace-keeping role in trouble-spots like East Timor.

The Spirit of Anzac,
Alan Moir,
Sydney Morning Herald,
9 May 2001.

The Politics

In early September 2001, when Ansett Australia was jettisoned, the New Zealand government was accused, particularly in Australia, of dithering over assisting with the restructuring of Air New Zealand. The airline bought half of Ansett from TNT in 1996; the remaining 50 percent from News Corp. in early 2000 for an inflated amount. Inadequate due diligence complicated by poor company records, additional competition in Australian skies, the grounding of planes, greatly increased fuel costs, the need for fleet replacement, and overstaffing all contributed to Ansett's losses mounting out of control.

"This Is Your Captain",
Alan Moir,
Sydney Morning Herald,
10 September 2001.

The Economics

"The Australian coo-ee, the Australian buck-jumping horse, the Australian stock-whip, and wide-awake hat came into New Zealand pastoral life"

The surprising lack of trade with the Australian colonies in the years preceding Federation was one of the reasons the idea of New Zealand becoming the seventh state in the new Commonwealth raised more yawns than enthusiasm on both sides of the Tasman. Also, those New Zealanders who thought about it believed that their's was a more caring and economically just society.

There had, of course, been a lively flow of goods and people back and forth in the early years of the nineteenth century. In 1830, 28 ships carried flax, pork, potatoes, and maize, grown by Maori who displayed both impressive entrepreneurial flair and the necessary agricultural skills, across the Tasman to Sydney. In 1840, the 2000 or so European settlers pepper-potted around New Zealand were mostly from New South Wales. With a head start of a half century or more, Australia's eastern colonies helped provision the first enclaves of arriving British settlers during their first struggling years. There was, in return, a demand for grain, tallow and timber in Sydney.

Unquestionably, the beginnings of New Zealand sheep farming had a definite Australian stamp to them. Many of the first runholders had sweated through their sheep farming apprenticeships in New South Wales or Victoria. William Pember Reeves

The Economics

wrote: "Coming to Canterbury, Otago, and Nelson, they [Australian squatters] taught the new settlers to look to wool and meat, rather than to oats and wheat, for profit and progress. The Australian *coo-ee*, the Australian buck-jumping horse, the Australian stock-whip, and wide-awake hat came into New Zealand pastoral life, together with much cunning in dodging land-laws, and a sovereign contempt for small areas." For New Zealand sheep farmers, the mechanics of funding an industry and marketing the product did not have to be re-invented. Most important, Australian stud farms provided the merinos that stocked the early runs.

Yet a potent brew of reasons resulted in sheep farming developing very differently in New Zealand. In Australia, with vast areas and mediocre fertility, an avaricious breed of financier-pastoralists occupied, leased and then bought immense holdings. It was not unusual for a single pastoralist to control 20 or more runs each totaling 30-50,000 acres. A half century later, shifts in political thinking, reaction to the Australian experience and the largely egalitarian impulses that had brought many of the first settlers to New Zealand provided an effective barrier to wholesale monopolies in land or anything else. This led to the primacy of the family farm and a political and economic system that was to lead to one of the world's first and most comprehensive welfare states.

During the 1860s, thriving on the east coasts of both islands, sheep numbers in New Zealand had quadrupled to nearly 10 million. In 1861, following the finds in California and Australia, the first substantial goldfield was discovered in Otago. In that year alone, 17,000 gold-hungry miners poured into that province from Australia. Not surprisingly, 60 percent of the country's growing export trade in gold and wool went to, or was trans-shipped from, the sizeable concentrations of population building up on Australia's eastern seaboard.

The growth in sheep numbers, and then dairy herds in the North Island, continued unabated. With wool prices and exports peaking and definite limits to the market for rendered down mutton, over-production was a looming dilemma before the timely appearance of refrigeration, pioneered in shipments from Australia. From the mid-1880s meat exports climbed rapidly; refrigeration plus the centrifugal separator gave a similar boost to butter and cheese.

Refrigeration offered economic salvation for New Zealand, but was only one option for Australia with its much larger domestic market and growing awareness of very considerable mineral wealth. As

The Economics

"Tie me Kangaroo down, Sport…"

The NAFTA Agreement, signed in 1966, made a start to freeing up trade between New Zealand and Australia, but over the next 17 years the ratio was generally strongly in the latter's favour.

"Tie me Kangaroo down, Sport …",
Gordon Minhinnick,
New Zealand Herald,
5 October 1967.

The Economics

historian Erik Olsen has written: "New Zealand ... became the Empire's farm at about the point when Australia set out to industrialise." A faltering of the Australian rural economy in the early 1890s was nudged towards stagnation by a long, cruel drought that decimated sheep and cattle numbers. There was production enough to feed the fast-growing cities, but not the necessity, family farm enthusiasm, or ready finance for agriculture that quickly transformed New Zealand into a leading manufacturer and exporter of meat and dairy products.

By 1900 New Zealand had settled comfortably and profitably into its role as Britain's meat, butter and cheese larder. These were, of course, agricultural commodities that Australia was self-sufficient in. As the details of Federation were being finalised, New Zealand's preoccupation was with its economic lifeline stretching 12,000 miles to the north rather than with its nearest neighbour, a mere 1200 miles to the west. Direct trade across the Tasman shrank further as the federal tariff on imports began to bite after the Anglo-Boer War and the easing of Australia's drought. But there was, in effect, a common labour market and banking system, and some self-interested co-operation when arguing Britain's lofty trade pronouncements.

By 1911 there was more cultivated land in New Zealand than in the whole of Australia. By 1927 only 6 percent of New Zealand's exports went across the Tasman and a paltry 2.9 percent of Australia's were shipped the other way – and this despite the first tentative attempts at a preferential trade agreement in 1922.

The two countries shared similar economic problems during the depression years, with unemployment at unprecedented levels. New Zealand's Reserve Bank, set up in 1934, was an understandable attempt to more closely control a currency that had long been tied to the Australian pound. In Australia, devaluation was described as an instrument of economic adjustment; in New Zealand, the newly elected Labour government was more comfortable with the rhetoric of sharing the economic burden more equitably. Overall, Australia came through the depression years in better shape because, with its mineral wealth and the evolution of companies like BHP (which became a significant steel producer), there was more opportunity for import substitution.

Grumpiness characterised the economic relationship during the inter-war period, although there was agreement on some issues, generally

The Economics

"Come off it—10 kits of category A kumaras equal one category B kangaroo any day."

New Zealand trade minister Lance Adams-Schneider and his Australian counterpart Doug Anthony confronting the reality of NAFTA. Free trade applied only to a limited range of 'Schedule A' items, mainly raw materials, and few of them agricultural. It was agreed on one occasion, with due solemnity, that the addition of sea water to the list of tariff free items would not harm producers or manufacturers in either country.

"Come off it ...",
Malcolm Evans,
New Zealand Herald,
6 April 1977.

The Economics

linked to the system of British Imperial Preferences. There was a history of Australia placing restrictions and embargoes on New Zealand potatoes and apples, and there was an unwelcome increase of the tariff on butter in 1927. In turn, New Zealand prohibited Australian fruit and vegetable imports in 1932, alleging a fruit-fly 'threat', and was exercised by an increasingly unequal trade balance and the embarrassment of importers preferring heavily devalued Australian goods, which put the cosy reciprocal trading arrangements with Britain under some pressure.

New Zealand's first Labour government promoted industrial development as an antidote to depression vulnerability. In 1938, when Labour brought in import licensing and exchange controls to insulate the economy, and the Social Security Act to insulate the family, the political and economic agenda launched by the Liberals in the 1890s was essentially complete. Australian governments, whatever their stripe, had been more pragmatic, aiming at full employment and a relatively egalitarian wage structure within a regulated, low tax economy. There were then, and subsequently, marked differences in the levels of public expenditure in the two countries.

The Canberra Pact, signed by Australia and New Zealand in 1944, contained encouraging phrases about economic co-operation, but there was little of it until the early 1960s. In part, this was because primary produce exports from both countries were cossetted from the realities of the post-war world by British bulk purchasing agreements for lamb, butter, cheese, wheat, sugar and wool that were hurriedly agreed in 1939 and continued undisturbed until the mid-1950s. By the early 1960s, though, it was clear that, sooner or later, Britain was going to join the EEC and history and sentiment would no longer be sufficient to justify special trading relationships.

Despite its name, the New Zealand Australia Free Trade Agreement (NAFTA), signed in 1966, was only partially what it claimed to be. It was given impetus from the New Zealand side, Britain's flirting with Europe aside, by the maturing of the country's pine forests and the need to shore up a substantial market for the anticipated bounty of wood pulp and newsprint.

Free trade applied only to a limited range of 'Schedule A' items; risking the survival of local industries was not an option. Import licensing remained central to New Zealand's economic

The Economics

Political boosting of NAFTA's success took considerable sleight of hand, but by the late 1970s it was clear that it had not broken down the substantial trade barriers between the two countries.

NAFTA,
Peter Bromhead,
Auckland Star,
10 April 1979.

The Economics

management and the agreement was top heavy with safeguards and escape clauses. If nothing else, though, NAFTA had demonstrated that trade in commodities produced in both countries could be freed without dire consequences.

Certainly, political inhibitions were now sufficiently relaxed for the two countries to sign up to Closer Economic Relations (CER) in 1982. With remarkably little haggling, the result was a genuine free trade area. Comprehensive from the beginning, the arrangement was reviewed three times up to 1995, and since then has been a focus of annual trade ministers' meetings. CER has achieved its primary aims of boosting free trade and increasing overall trade by removing barriers and providing fairer competition. Knotty issues like customs, business law, standards, and quarantine regulations have been progressively sorted out. Australia is New Zealand's biggest market; New Zealand is Australia's fourth largest.

Cartoon by Al Nisbet.

There has been talk, perhaps inevitably, about economic union and a common currency. These prospects particularly exercise the minds of New Zealand politicians. Their reasoning goes something like this: we have limited economic sovereignty now – four of our five banks are Australian-owned, head offices are moving across the Tasman and our Stock Exchange is increasingly sidelined – but economic union would be on Australian terms and a common currency would be the Australian dollar. Which sounds like a short hop and a step to political union.

There is already more economic co-operation than between any two other countries, the argument goes, so why look to add complications? Business has already made the mental adjustment and treats the two countries as one market – sometimes with unfortunate consequences when a Sydney-based marketing manager decides how something will be sold in Tokoroa. Others claim that talk about economic union is now irrelevant – globalisation means, they say, that *Fortune* 500

The Economics

Cartoonist Trace Hodgson was unduly harsh in his view of CER's effectiveness. Two-way trade soared from about $2.2 billion in 1982 to $9.81 billion in 1998. CER made more progress in its first three years than NAFTA did in 17.

The evolution of CER,
Trace Hodgson,
N.Z. Listener,
12 December 1987.

53

The Economics

companies call the shots, with the role of governments reduced to smoothing the way in front and tidying up behind.

All this aside, probably the greatest success of the Australia-New Zealand economic relationship has been a movement of people back and forth as constant as the tides lapping both sides of the Tasman. Social historian Rollo Arnold called it the 'Perennial Interchange'. There was a net gain of 154,000 Australians moving to live and work in New Zealand between 1858 and 1965. The situation has been dramatically different since then, particularly as New Zealanders realised that better economic prospects across the Tasman were not a temporary phenomenon.

Today, a million and a half people criss-cross the Tasman each year, with a sharply increasing number of New Zealanders deciding to remain on the other side. There are about 435,000 New Zealanders permanently in Australia, but only 55,000 Australians returning the compliment. There are now more Maori in New South Wales than in the whole of the South Island. New Zealand has worried about losing some of its 'best' and 'brightest' to Australia; Canberra's concerns have focused more on growing welfare costs. Changes to reciprocal agreements will now mean less generous welfare concessions for New Zealanders arriving in Australia.

No amount of political spin can hide the fact that Australia's economy has left New Zealand's wallowing in its wake. They once had two of the highest standards of living in the world; Australia has stumbled a little, New Zealand has plummeted. New Zealand's economic growth has been 20 percent less than Australia's during the last two decades – the period of the evangelical transformation of the economy led by New-Right prophets Douglas and Richardson. Productivity and competitiveness have slumped by comparison and, during the same period, the gap in the average income in the two countries has widened to more than $NZ15,000. It is an economic trend unlikely to be reversed in the forseeable future.

The Economics

The Bank of New Zealand had lent speculatively and recklessly to some of the 1980s entrepreneurs, corporate cowboys on a scale that Australia's Ned Kelly would never have imagined possible. After their over-hyped companies collapsed following the 1987 stock market crash, successive Labour and National governments bailed out the bank to the collective tune of $1.3 billion. Calls for a public inquiry were stifled by its secretive sale to National Australia Bank in late 1992.

"Hey Boss ...",
Chicane,
PSA Journal,
March-April 1989.

The Economics

New Zealand introduced a rigid, New-Right economic regime in the mid-1980s, beginning with 'Rogernomics' and reinforced by 'Ruthomania'. Australian policies were more pragmatic, and driven more by commonsense than ideology. There, the government continued to play a role in areas where, across the Tasman, responsibility was handed holus-bolus to the private sector. Australia's economy thrived while New Zealand's shrivelled.

Australia-New Zealand,
Bob Brockie,
National Business Review,
11 September 1997

The Economics

New Zealand's finance minister Roger Douglas introduced a 10 percent goods and services tax (GST) in October 1986, convincing the Labour Party it would reduce tax avoidance by the rich and provide revenue for redistribution. Although the 'benefits' of GST, later increased to 12.5 percent, and other aspects of Douglas's 'trickle down' theory proved elusive, Australia, while rejecting many of New Zealand's more extreme economic policies, adopted a version of GST in 1998.

"Yeah cute …", Garrick Tremain, *Otago Daily Times*, 5 October 1998.

The Economics

Although the gut Australian reaction to the flood of New Zealanders across the Tasman is that the Kiwis are dole-bludging surfies, statistics suggest that, on average, there are more of them in work, earning more and paying more tax than the locals. Nevertheless, completely unrestricted movement back and forth across the Tasman ended when Australia introduced a two-year stand-down period before arriving New Zealanders could qualify for most benefits. In 2000, the New Zealand government contributed over $169 million towards Kiwi welfare costs in Australia.

"Howard's getting Clark to pay …",
Garrick Tremain,
Otago Daily Times,
29 February 2000.

The Economics

Despite the 'blossoming' of free trade between the two countries under CER, New Zealand sees the continuing exclusion of apples as another devious Australian ploy. The Australians say New Zealand has fireblight, a bacterial disease; New Zealand apple growers claim it attacks blossoms and the fruit is unaffected. The Australian government says it's a quarantine issue; New Zealand calls it a restrictive trade practice. The situation has been further muddied by recent claims that fireblight has been discovered in Australia.

Aussie Protectionism, Jim Hubbard, *Hawke's Bay Today,* 20 October 2000.

The Economics

The possum, introduced from Australia in 1858, has long been a noxious animal in New Zealand, costing the taxpayer hundreds of millions a year in a seemingly futile control programme. New Zealanders are not markedly more popular in Australia and in February 2001 the two governments signed an agreement under which new arrivals will have to gain permanent residency, in competition with other applicants, before qualifying for the dole and most benefits.

"While we're on the subject of bludgers …", Tom Scott, *Evening Post*, 27 February 2001.

> WHILE WE'RE ON THE SUBJECT OF BLUDGERS THAT CROSS THE TASMAN, AUSSIE TAXPAYERS COULD PICK UP THE TAB FOR THIS BLOKE...

The Sport

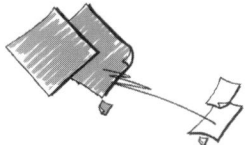

"On the hilly side of the Tasman, a rugby loss is a disaster of major earthquake proportions"

Traditionally, neighbouring countries have got angst out of their systems by going to war. Australia and New Zealand 'play' sport instead. Everything from lawn bowls to sheep shearing 'test' matches are hyped as 'world championships', even if very few countries in the world have even heard of a particular sport.

There is something to be said, psychologically speaking, for knocking the hell out of the other country in sporting encounters and then companionably comparing bruises over a beer or three. It could also be argued that it is very strange to put so much passion, pride, time, effort and money into chasing variously shaped balls around variously sized spaces. But we are talking gut feelings here, not logic or reason.

Sport was an important component of frontier life during Australasia's early European years. With shorter working hours than in the 'old country', and usually some coins jingling in the pocket, the opportunity to play sport gave practical expression to 'Jack is as good as his master' attitudes, and a sports ground was invariably one of the first facilities in a new township. And what could be more natural than an active preoccupation with sport in highly physical environments where men usually

The Sport

outnumbered women?

There were differences, though, in the way sport developed in the two countries. In New Zealand, the same instincts that led to the wholesale introduction of deer to hunt and gorse to gaze at resulted in the easy acceptance of rugby, played at school by many of the young colony's leaders. But it was rugby with an egalitarian difference; everyone played and Maori participation was welcomed. Rugby was part of the mortar that gave a unity of purpose to small isolated communities.

Across the Tasman, rugby's links to the establishment that had packed off Australia's first unwilling emigrants to Botany Bay was a seriously inhibiting factor. It was sufficient reason, along with inter-state rivalries, to look elsewhere. The Victorians invented Australian Rules and exported it around the continent. New South Wales and Queensland favoured rugby league, developed in England's industrial midlands.

It is a moot point, much debated by social historians, which was more formative in the first stirrings of national identity in New Zealand – the All Blacks' first, almost unblemished tour of Britain in 1905 or the Expeditionary Force heroics at Gallipoli in 1915. The truth is probably that both were important. Australia took similar pride in its sporting and wartime achievements.

But at bottom, for many Australians and New Zealanders the celebration of sporting prowess is about as close as they get to expressing views about national pride and identity.

As Britain's South Seas colonies they had been lumped together as 'Australasia', and had even used the term themselves. Tennis, true to its genteel cream flannels and afternoon teas tradition, kept the idea alive until the early 1920s, with New Zealand's Anthony Wilding and Australia's Norman Brookes winning the Davis Cup on three occasions before the outbreak of the First World War.

But in other sports, early nationalistic stirrings, then the Federation of the Australian colonies, helped intensify trans-Tasman rivalry. No history has listed sporting clashes as a reason for lack of enthusiasm in both countries about New Zealand joining the Federation, but it would certainly have robbed innumerable sporting codes of decades of spirited, sometimes acrimonious, international fixtures. The trans-Tasman sporting calendar has been a considerable boon to shipping companies and, more recently, to the airline industry.

It has to be admitted that New Zealand has taken

The Sport

Ninety years ago New Zealand was acquiring a reputation for its breeding of race horses and their fleetness of foot. At regular intervals, New Zealand horses have continued to win the major Australian races – the Melbourne and Caulfield Cups and W. S. Cox Plate among others. The first New Zealand-bred Melbourne Cup winner was Martini Henri in 1883. Australian owners and trainers are routinely prominent buyers at New Zealand yearling sales.

New Zealand,
Lionel Lindsay,
The Bulletin,
c.1907.

63

The Sport

this sporting competitiveness more seriously, as with most aspects of the relationship. It used to be claimed that Australia and New Zealand had more world-class sports people per capita than anywhere else. It remains true for Australia; it's doubtful whether it ever was for New Zealand, except for brief purple patches of middle distance running glory and regular success in niche sports like squash, ocean racing and things equestrian, including the business of breeding horse flesh. Certainly New Zealand generally has an uphill battle when it takes the field, literally or metaphorically, against Australia today, and this does nothing to lessen the intensity of feeling. But if there is a David v. Goliath aspect to most competitive situations New Zealand finds itself in, sport is probably the one where its sling-shots will count most.

On the hilly side of the Tasman a rugby loss is a disaster of major earthquake proportions. There is national mourning, oceans of printer's ink post-mortem the result, picking through the reasons with more intensity than economists scrutinize budgets, and then black caps are donned to pass sentence. Political science may be no more science than reading tea leaves, but there is growing evidence of a direct relationship between the government's political poll performance and the current fortunes of the All Blacks.

"Why are our national moods so bound up in the particular success with which 15 men in black chase a piece of leather?" asked historian Jock Phillips about New Zealand's early and long obsession with rugby that rivals Australia's for cricket. Well, everybody played it. Young farmers who hefted fence posts and upended sheep during the week made tough, rampaging forwards on Saturdays. As important, in terms of being the best in the world, very few other countries played rugby.

It was a minority sport in the British Isles, apart from Wales. In Australia it was the preserve of private schools in New South Wales and Queensland, and far greater numbers played Australian Rules and league. South Africa was off the rugby stage during the 1980s, when, for a while, the All Blacks were clearly No. 1. The new professional era has hugely boosted playing numbers in traditional rugby countries and excited interest in the unlikeliest of places. Today, there are more rugby players in Japan than in either New Zealand or Australia. In the future, the All Blacks will continue to beat most other teams – on a good day.

This is possibly more than can be claimed for the New Zealand cricket team. There is a residual bitterness that still flares up occasionally, most

The Sport

In 1921, the All Blacks played four 'at home' matches. Against South Africa they won two out of three test matches – the first played between the two countries. Then they suffered the considerable indignity of being beaten 0-17 by New South Wales. Trevor Lloyd is widely credited as being the first artist to use the kiwi to symbolise New Zealand.

Nil (desperandum), Trevor Lloyd, *original wash drawing*, 1921.

The Sport

famously in February 1981 on the day of the never-to-be-forgiven under-arm bowling incident, that the Australians so long treated New Zealand cricket with the disdain it possibly merited. New Zealand played its first cricket test, against England, in 1930; Australia deigned to play one test in Wellington 16 years later. This act of benevolence by the masters of world cricket was to suffice for a further 27 years.

It is probably in netball, one of the most popular women's sports on both sides of the Tasman, that New Zealand and Australian teams are most evenly matched, well ahead of the relatively few other countries playing competitively. Now, frenetic television hyping is giving the game iconic status in New Zealand. Interestingly, it is still played by young women with day jobs.

Today, more and more high profile sport is professional. Key elements of the trans-Tasman professionalisation of sport can be traced directly to the boardroom feuding of Australian media barons Kerry Packer and Rupert Murdoch. In the late 1970s, with the willing compliance of a cricket-mad public, Packer invented the one-day game to boost local content and ratings on his TV network. Before long, breathless revelations about the amounts paid to Aussie Rules footballers, league players and cricketers jostled for front page tabloid space with the traditional parade of sex scandals.

In the early 1990s, Rupert Murdoch, now nominally an American, targeted rugby. The roots of Murdoch's global media empire remain in Australia and it was from there, as a way of helping satisfy the greedy programming appetite of multi-channel pay-TV, that he offered the major rugby-playing nations very large dollops of money for TV rights, turning hundreds of players into professionals and fast-tracking the stars to millionaire status.

TV-led professionalism has turned Australia and New Zealand's major spectator sports into businesses, with the same stresses and strains as everyone else fighting for market share. The rivalries might remain amongst players and spectators, but to the marketers in control the two countries are now a single trans-Tasman TV audience. The Super 12 and tri-nations competitions are designed to give a maximum amount of screen-time to the Southern Hemisphere's rugby heavyweights. In soccer and league, New Zealand teams have joined the premier Australian competitions. And every week league commentators mangle the names of the growing number of Maori playing for Australian teams.

Australia's sustained sporting success seems to

The Sport

In 1972 the All Blacks played a home series against Australia, winning all three tests by convincing margins. Nevile Lodge's *Sports Post* cartoons, that eventually filled the front cover of the *Evening Post's* early Saturday evening sports edition, had an enthusiastic following in the Wellington region. With test match results not known until just before press time, the cartoonist became adept at drawing three similar versions each time – for a win, draw and loss.

First Test,
Nevile Lodge,
Sports Post,
19 August 1972.

The Sport

be based in various measures on a benign climate, a certain mental toughness, and growing national wealth that can fund an Institute of Sport approach to developing talent. On the other hand, New Zealand has looked for sporting dominance, seemingly so important to New Zealand's self confidence, in the unlikeliest places.

Messing about in boats is a predictable enough pastime in both Australia and New Zealand, with their unending coastlines and fine harbours. But the America's Cup is of a totally different stripe: salt-water jousting among the super-wealthy.

In as striking a departure from their egalitarian pasts as can be imagined, both Australia and New Zealand have coveted the 'Auld Mug'. There were striking similarities and one fundamental difference in the approaches taken. Two self-made tycoons, Alan Bond and Michael Fay, spearheaded the Australian and New Zealand Cup campaigns respectively. Of course, they did so for reasons that had more to do with corporate image-making than the exhilaration of salt spray in the eyes. Bond succeeded in 1983 and ended up in prison; Fay showed that New Zealand could win one day and left for Switzerland. For those who savour ironies, Fay was knighted for his patriotic pursuit of yachting glory while he was one of the principal beneficiaries of the sell-off of great slabs of the country's state sector to overseas interests.

Australia won the America's Cup and then showed little concern at losing it again. Australia did, after all, have other sporting fish to fry. But when New Zealand won in 1995 there was a grim, dogged determination, from the cabinet table down, that it would be retained at all costs. It was a matter of National Importance. The America's Cup might be raced over the horizon, and well beyond the comprehension of most citizens, but nationalistic fervour was duly manufactured with a massive PR campaign and blanket TV coverage that surpassed previous records for monotony.

Of course, the America's Cup is really big business dressed up to look jaunty and nautical. On the credit side it has tidied up downtown Auckland and put New Zealand on the luxury boat-building map. At the same time, the massive sponsorship amounts are more than the country spends collectively on every other imaginable sport from archery to underwater hockey, all of which New Zealanders actually play and watch.

In the end, there is no denying that sport plays a major part in defining the Australian and New Zealand psyche. Nor that the Aussies win a great deal more often.

The Sport

The results of trans-Tasman rugby tests are followed more closely than general election results – at least in New Zealand. A long list of excuses was being lined up – fractured jaw and hand, pulled hamstrings, damaged knees, neck and back, and concussion – before the final and deciding 1980 test, won handily by Australia.

"Having to field all those injured players …",
Nevile Lodge,
Evening Post,
11 July 1980.

69

The Sport

In February 1981, New Zealand needed to hit a six off the last ball to tie a crucial game in the World Series cricket finals. The Australians' underarm bowl reverberates today, a convenient symbol for a sense of moral superiority over a much larger 'uncouth' neighbour. Even NZ Prime Minister Muldoon got into the act, branding the Aussies as "yellow" as their one-day uniforms.

A Feather In Their Cap,
Peter Bromhead,
Auckland Star,
2 February 1981.

The Sport

In 1983, when the Australians prised the America's Cup – the 25th challenge – away from the United States, New Zealand, with its strong yachting tradition and a string of successes to boost confidence, was already casting a covetous eye at the 'Auld Mug'.

Kiwi Wins Melbourne Cup,
Eric Heath,
The Dominion,
3 November 1983.

The Sport

New Zealand had very lean pickings at the 1994 Commonwealth Games held in Victoria, Canada. Australia finished the Games with 50 medals (including 22 golds) while New Zealand managed 10 – only two of them gold.

"A Heart-warming Sight …",
Garrick Tremain,
Otago Daily Times,
29 August 1994.

A HEART-WARMING SIGHT AT THESE GAMES IS THE LITTLE KIWI GUIDING HIS NOW SIGHT-IMPAIRED FRIEND AROUND THE CITY

The Sport

In 1996, to the consternation of some, an Australian, Steve Rixon, was appointed coach of the New Zealand cricket team. While the underarm bowling incident still rankled, it was hoped that an Australian might inject a little more of the killer instinct needed to improve the generally disappointing Black Caps' record.

"Aussie Coach!",
Al Nisbet,
The Press,
26 July 1996.

The Sport

With barely contained fury, the New Zealand media regularly points out the 'co-incidence' of leading Kiwi players, 'sin-binned' in Australia's NRL competition, being banned for periods that extend just beyond the date of the national side's next test match against their trans-Tasman rivals.

"Look Cobber …", Garrick Tremain, *Otago Daily Times*, 28 March 1999.

> LOOK COBBER, WE'VE VIEWED THE FOOTAGE AND YA DEFINITELY BUMPED THE BLOKE!…

> YOU KIWIS GOTTA LEARN THAT AUSSIE LEAGUE WON'T TOLERATE THAT SORTA STUFF! YOU'RE HEREBY SUSPENDED…

> JEEZ BLUE, HOW LONG TILL THE KIWI TEST?
> 4½ WEEKS

> … FOR 5 WEEKS!… NEXT!

74

Shane Warne might be an Aussie sporting icon, but on the other side of the Tasman he's more likely to be portrayed as a prime 'destroyer' of New Zealand's fragile cricketing pride. The media pounced when he swore at a young fan who photographed him smoking during a match in Wellington. It was, apparently, something he was being paid in Australia not to do. The public was suitably outraged.

Warne-ing, Tom Scott, *Evening Post*, 24 February 2000.

The Culture

"What do 'Advance Australia Fair' and 'God Defend New Zealand' say about their respective national psyches?"

Culturally, there has always been a mutual trans-Tasman ambivalence.

This rivalry between New Zealanders and Australians, and occasional downright hostility, puzzles people from other countries who can rarely tell them apart. This, of course, tends to infuriate New Zealanders all the more, especially when Californians, who would be hard-pressed to name the states on their own country's eastern seaboard, say: "Noo Zealand, sure, that's those pretty islands in Sydney Harbour".

New Zealanders and Australians are really very similar, but work hard at enlarging and distorting the differences. Why on earth do they do it? The *NZ Herald* may well have been right when it editorialised after a recent bout of anti-Australianism: "As a people most of the world cannot tell New Zealanders and Australians apart. From a distance our accents, interests and mannerisms are virtually undistinguishable. Perhaps perversely, that explains our antagonism. Our identity can all too easily disappear when Australia is prominent".

This business of identity has long been a preoccupation on both sides of the Tasman, and history has coloured the search. For a long time

The Culture

> MEN OF THE AMERICAN ANTARCTIC OPERATION WILL TAKE THEIR LEAVE IN SYDNEY BECAUSE CHRISTCHURCH IS CONSIDERED TOO DULL... NEWS

"Shucks! What do folks do with their time in this Burg?"

For many years 'Operation Deep Freeze', the logistical arm of the United States' Antarctic programme, was based in Christchurch. There were up to 100 air trips to McMurdo and back between October and February each year. In the 1950s visitors noted that New Zealand closed down at weekends, so it was not surprising that 'rest and recreation' for Deep Freeze servicemen was moved from Christchurch to the much racier Sydney.

"Shucks!",
Neil Lonsdale,
Auckland Star,
16 August 1956.

The Culture

New Zealand was smothered by its obsession with being the 'Britain of the South Seas', with acclimatisation societies trying their level best to create, in the countryside and in the rivers, facsimilies of what had been left behind in England and Scotland.

Anthony Trollope wrote in his 1873 book *Australia and New Zealand*: "The New Zealander among John Bulls is the most John Bullish. He admits the supremacy of England to any place in the world, only he is more English than every Englishman at home." As late as the 1990s older New Zealanders could be heard talking, in reverential tones, about 'Home'. The Gallipoli campaign is widely seen as a defining point in the evolution of New Zealand nationhood. But, as historian Jock Phillips has written, "The Kiwis were fighting on the far side of the globe as part of an Australian force within an Imperial Army." Perhaps the decision not to join the Federation of Australian colonies was, in fact, the first really defining moment in the quest for a separate identity.

The first European settlers in Australia, most of them unwilling guests of Britain's brutal penal service, were concerned about survival. The fight to survive was often fuelled by a hatred of a country that sent them, without return tickets, to the bottom of the world. Perhaps, when you begin with few expectations and things turn out so much better, you become an optimistic nation, a 'lucky country'.

Sam Neill, international actor of Anglo-Irish parentage and New Zealand upbringing, and now a passionate South Islander has said: "New Zealanders are dull, decent and phlegmatic". Bob Catley, Australian politician turned political scientist, has summed up the stereotypes as neatly as anyone. New Zealanders see Australians as brash and uncultured. Australians, when they think of them at all, view New Zealanders as under-performing, sheep-loving losers, two hours in front and 20 years behind.

Stereotypes do have, along with cliches, a certain broad-brush veracity to them, but they tend to be gross exaggerations. Overall, it is probably easier to describe the factual similarities between the two countries than the mythologised differences. As J. D. B. Miller, an Australian political scientist, has written: " ... they are both European settlements on the outskirts of Asia; they are petty-bourgeois communities with an intense

The Culture

There has been a long tradition of sheep shearers moving back and forth across the Tasman, but New Zealanders, with their hard work and more advanced techniques, provided unpopular competition in outback Australia.

"Caught 'Im With A Wide One",
Eric Heath,
The Dominion,
16 October 1984.

79

regard for their standards of living; they have very close affinities with European civilisation and its development in the United States; and they cannot be easily assimilated to any Asian life-style ..."

There are, undoubtedly, differences, and the geography of the two countries may have tempered national traits. Australia is huge, a country of physical and climatic extremes. Perhaps a never-ending landscape breeds a more expansive outlook? New Zealand is a narrow, cramped chain of small islands. Possibly there is a connection to the 'reserved' and 'retiring' labels many New Zealanders are happy to acknowledge.

Of course, there is one fundamental and growing cultural difference between the two countries. Australia's Aboriginal beginnings have little significance for most citizens today; in New Zealand, by dint of history, a treaty and the reality of fast-growing numbers, there is a vigorous revival of Maori culture. In a generation's time, Maori will be 25 percent of the New Zealand population, and the country's identity will have a distinctly Polynesian flavour to it.

Differences also have something to do with the much higher percentage of Irish in the Australian cultural mix compared to the stodgier English and Scots who packed the first immigrant ships to New Zealand. The differences are now greater following the influx of southern Europeans into Australia following the Second World War. New Zealand's European population has remained more homogeneous, possibly explaining the well-defined self-deprecating streak in the country's sense of humour. This can be a positive virtue, says Christchurch theologian and writer John Bluck, except when it contributes to the black cloud of national pessimism he sees hovering over New Zealand. Australian literary and popular mythology often focuses on 'mateship', while New Zealand seems to have been unduly absorbed by the 'man alone' theme.

In a nutshell, Australia and Australians generally seem as confident as New Zealand and New Zealanders are reticent.

This confidence – or lack of it – is apparent in many ways. It's there, subtly, in the countries' anthems. What do 'Advance Australia Fair' and 'God Defend New Zealand' say about their respective national psyches?

The jokes are less subtle. New Zealand ones presume a sort of cultural and intellectual superiority that is really a whopping inferiority

The Culture

'Footrot Flats', the strip cartoon saga featuring Wal, 'the dog' and a cast of characters from rural New Zealand has been widely syndicated in Australia. In 1991, cartoonist Murray Ball, after holidaying in the Northern Territory's Kakada National Park, decided to send Wal and 'the dog' to visit as well.

'Footrot Flats', Murray Ball, 1991.

81

The Culture

complex. Australians are less refined and clearly less intelligent. There are endless variations to the standard joke. "Question: What are the four longest years of an Australian's life? Answer: The fifth form." Sir Robert Muldoon's much quoted "New Zealanders moving to Australia raise the IQ on both sides of the Tasman" says more about the populist politician than it does about the remarkably peaceful and purposeful migrations between the two countries stretching back well over a century. Muldoon's quip: "Now I know why the Australian cricket uniforms are yellow", after the 1981 'under-arm bowling' incident, probably struck a more responsive cord among New Zealanders. Australia's convict beginnings must by now be deeply submerged in that country's gene pool, but New Zealanders are quick to see, for example, a certain symmetry between rock-breaking felons and the 'sledging' tactics their modern-day cricketers are noted for.

Australian jokes about New Zealand, and 'Poms' for that matter, are of quite another stripe. They are firmly cast in the dismissive mold. Question: "If a Pom and a Kiwi fall off the Sydney Harbour Bridge at the same time, which one will hit the water first? Answer: Who cares?" Indifference is probably the most cruel joke of all. At most New Zealand is a minor irritant, like the bush flies Kiwi cartoons have swarming around Aussie heads. New Zealand angst is really no match for Australian boredom.

The mystery of all this is that at Gallipoli Aussies and Kiwis were brothers-in-arms and today, in Earl's Court and other London haunts, they're best mates. It is at home, in the South Pacific, where the similarities are most obvious, that Australia and New Zealand often seem poles apart.

New Zealand's aggressive attitude is all the more puzzling considering so many Kiwis have close Australian connections - a grandfather in banking or insurance who climbed the promotional ladder via a move to one side of the Tasman or the other, a cousin whose shearing forays to Victoria and New South Wales led to marriage and permanent residence, a son or daughter building up corporate CVs and paying off student loans in Sydney or Melbourne, parents warming arthritic joints on the Queensland coast, or friends chasing bigger bucks in the construction industry.

Two prominent New Zealand writers at opposite ends of the literary spectrum – Frank

The Culture

NEW DINKUM OLYMPIC MASCOT NEEDED —*NEWS*

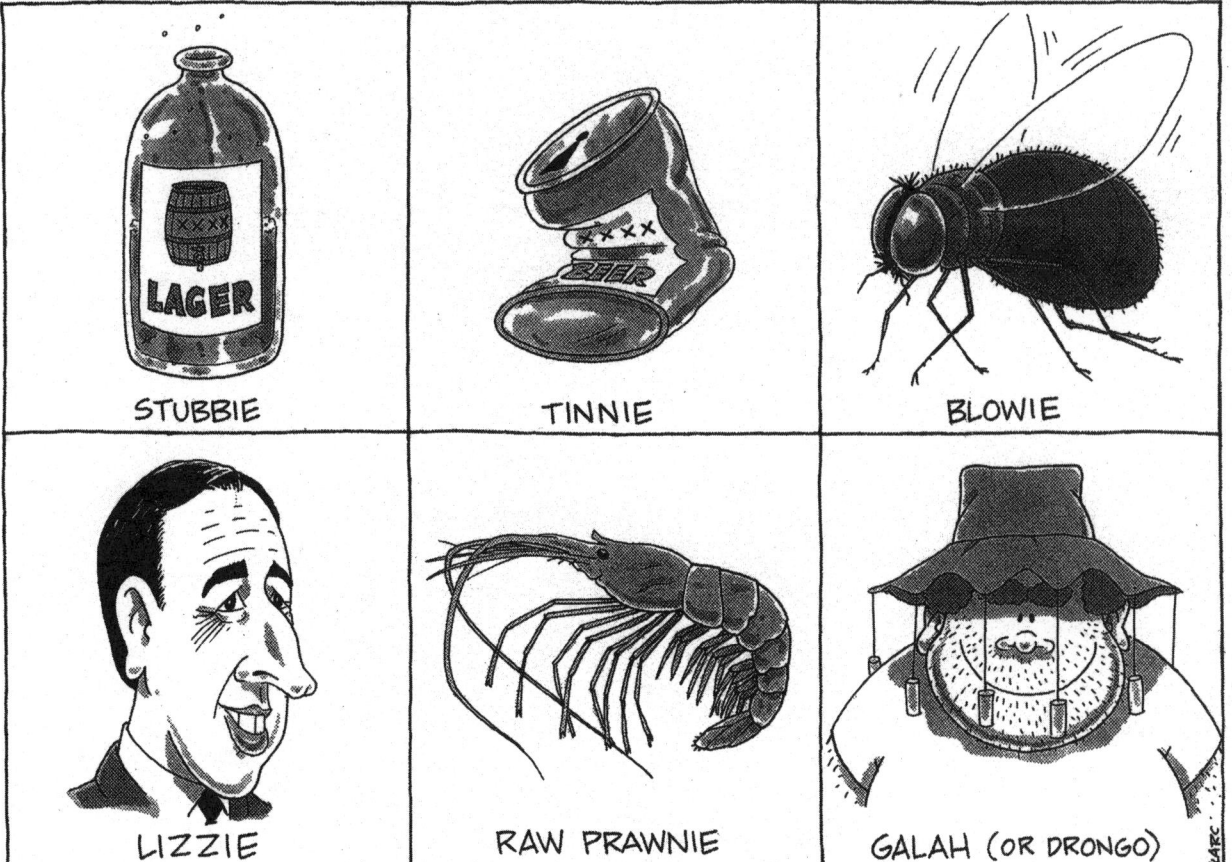

| STUBBIE | TINNIE | BLOWIE |
| LIZZIE | RAW PRAWNIE | GALAH (OR DRONGO) |

When the organisers called for mascot ideas for the Sydney Olympics in 2000, Auckland cartoonist Klarc came up with some 'dinkum' suggestions. More predictably, the Australians chose 'Ollie' the kookaburra, 'Syd' platypus and 'Millie', an echidna or, to the uninitiated, a spiny, insect-eating mammal.

Stubbie, Tinnie, Blowie …,
Klarc,
New Zealand Herald,
30 September 1993.

The Culture

Sargeson and Frank Anthony – looked to Australia for inspiration. Sargeson wrote about his debt to Henry Lawson and Anthony's popular 'Me and Gus' rural stereotypes owed a great deal to Australia's 'Dad and Dave', the backblocks family saga that was hugely popular for decades in books, and on radio, film and stage. Yet Murray Ball's 'Footrot Flats' cartoon strip, equally popular across the Tasman, owes nothing to Australian cartoonists, like Joliffe, who were major contributors to the outback mythology.

Often, though, it's as if there is a wall rather than a stretch of water between the two countries. In 1947, New Zealand writer A. R. D. Fairburn wrote that "looking at the state of cultural relations between Australia and New Zealand I can't help thinking of two shipwrecked Englishmen who lived together for years on a desert island without speaking, because they hadn't been introduced."

Three years earlier, an Australian, Nettie Palmer, wrote: "…it required assiduous curiosity on the part of an Australian would-be observer, helped out by something like a miracle, before any of us could find what was being done over there … Australian bookshops in general took no more interest in the books of New Zealand than in those of Nova Scotia."

This might have been written in 2001, a half a century and more later. In the era of instant communication, nothing has changed. Bookshops in both countries go to considerable lengths not to stock books from 'across the ditch'. The branch

Cartoon by Tom Scott.

The Culture

When New Zealanders are feeling really put upon by Australians there are two lines of attack guaranteed to brighten them up: Australia's penal settlement beginnings and the treatment of Aboriginals.

"See The Government ...", Garrick Tremain, *Otago Daily Times*, 20 December 1994.

offices of international publishing houses assiduously ignore each other. If New Zealand shops have skyscraper piles of the books of Colleen McCullough and Bryce Courtenay it is because they are international best-selling authors, not because they are Australian. And their books will come via London and New York, not Sydney.

Both countries look to North America and Europe, rarely to each other, for art exhibitions, opera and ballet companies, and symphony orchestras. Some cultural ties were, in fact, stronger in the past, at least for New Zealanders, many of whom were avid readers of Nevile Shute, Ion Idress and Frank Clune in the days before international bestsellerdom. New Zealand was also an integral part of an Australasian theatrical touring circuit, and for seven years from 1923 a special section of *Aussie*, a popular literary magazine, featured the work of a number of New Zealand writers and cartoonists.

Perhaps because much of the cultural traffic is one way – from pop singer Dinah Lee to satirist John Clarke – New Zealand is more than a little neurotic about preserving the identity of their icons. It's important to New Zealanders that the world, and particularly Aussies, know that Mrs Crowe gave birth to film star Russell in Wellington, Phar Lap found his coltish legs in Timaru, that the pavlova is a Kiwi culinary invention, film director Jane Campion grew up in the capital, and that Clarrie Grimmett, who spun some magical Australian cricketing victories, hailed from Dunedin.

The hard-nosed reality, though, is that New Zealand needs Australia a great deal and Australia needs New Zealand hardly at all. This, as Bob Catley puts it, is "the multi-dimensional and often unfathomable challenge which Australia poses to the New Zealand national psyche." A good indication of how much one country rates in the consciousness of another is a count of column centimetres of newspaper coverage or the minutes of TV time. In Australia New Zealand news rarely rates a passing mention, except of the grizzliest kind; New Zealand media gives lavish treatment to things Australian, particularly if there is an insult to brood over or a loss to gloat about.

How much of a coincidence is it, then, that Australia's master of theatrical invention Barry Humphries should equip his alter ego Dame Edna Everidge with Madge, a mousy, downtrodden, silent 'companion' – from New Zealand?

The Culture

In London or New York the locals often find it difficult to tell New Zealanders and Australians apart. This is a particularly sore point to some New Zealanders who still defer to the 'Queen's English' and Home Counties accents. To them there is a world of difference between how they and Australians speak and their vocabularies.

"Yeah Gidday Digger", Malcolm Evans, *New Zealand Herald*, 7 July 1998.

The Culture

There was consternation when 'Project Blue Sky', a consortium of producers, broadcasters and funding agencies, won the right for New Zealand productions to be included in Australian TV's local content quota. In the event, neither Australian fears nor New Zealand hopes have been realised. In 2000, the Seven, Nine and Ten networks screened a combined total of 8.9 hours of New Zealand programming.

"..Action!",
Alan Moir,
Sydney Morning Herald,
4 November 1999.

The Culture

It was disclosed early in 2001 that man generally and the kiwi specifically may have originated in Australia, with the kiwi migrating to New Zealand about 70 million years ago along the then-exposed Norfolk Ridge or Lord Howe Rise that linked the two countries. Man's beginnings are murkier, but Auckland cartoonist Malcolm Evans has his own evolutionary theory.

New Theory,
Malcolm Evans,
New Zealand Herald,
11 January 2001.

The Culture

Leaving aside the possum that was intentionally brought to New Zealand, one by-product of increasing trans-Tasman trade and tourism has been the arrival of Australians, including blowflies, spiders, mosquitoes and wasps, with no redeeming features.

One Real Threat Of Invasion,
Chris Slane,
N.Z. Listener,
21 April 2001

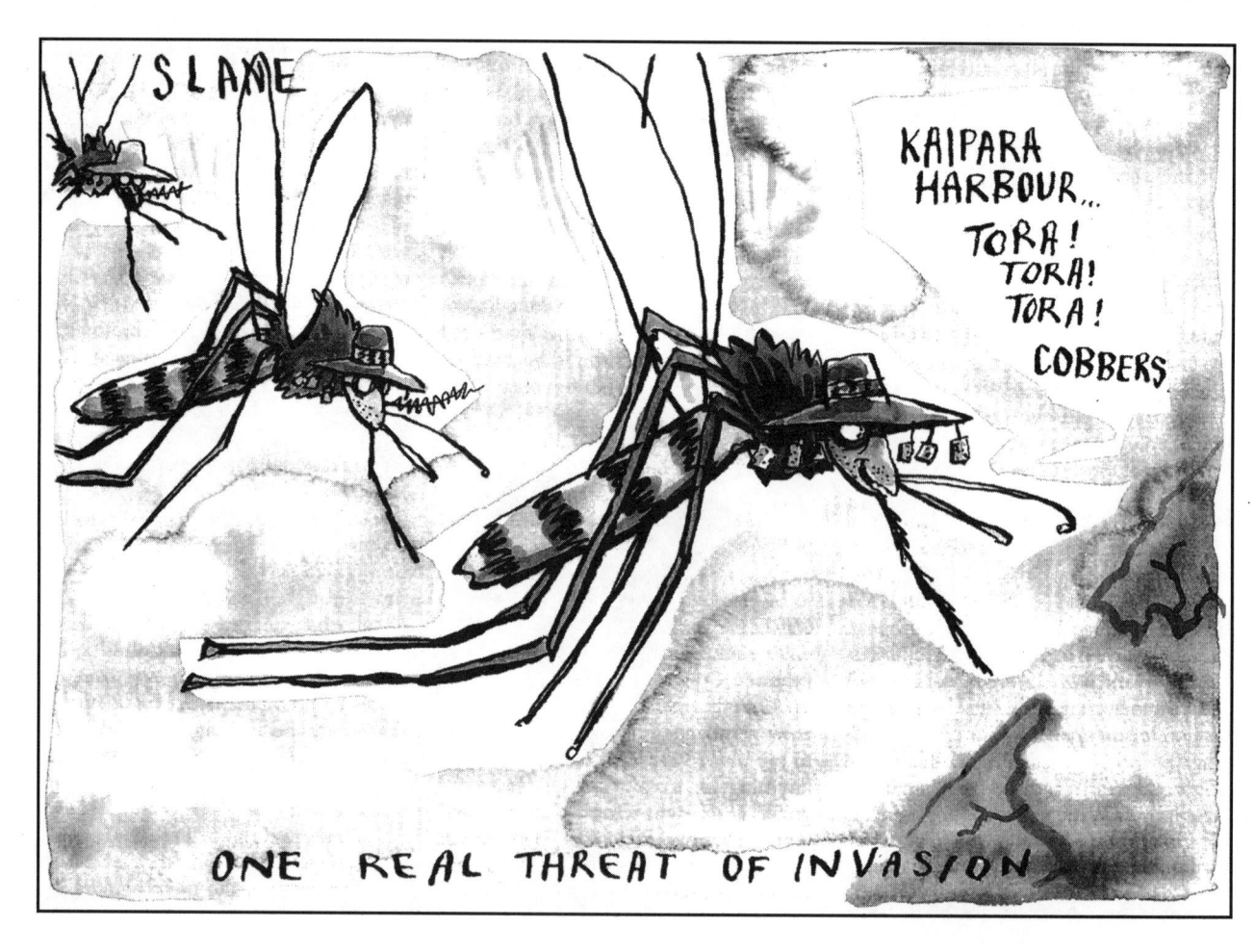

In September 2001, the Australian government's refusal to let 438 mainly Afghan refugees to land on Australian soil, after being rescued from a sinking ferry in the Indian Ocean by a Norwegian container ship, met with considerable public support on both sides of the Tasman. The New Zealand government's decision to assist by taking 150 of the refugees was not popular amongst 'red neck' listeners to talk-back radio in New Zealand.

"But Caller …",
Tom Scott,
Evening Post,
31 August 2001.

The References

Books

Bluck, John. *Killing Us Softly: Challenging the Kiwi Culture of Complaint*, Christchurch, 2001.
Catley, Bob. *Waltzing with Matilda*, Wellington, 2001.
Grant, Ian F. *The Unauthorized Version: A Cartoon History of New Zealand*, Auckland, 1980 (second, updated edition 1987).
Horsphol, Leslie. *The Story of Australia's Federation*, Sydney, 1985.
Laidlaw, Chris. *Rights of Passage*, Auckland, 1999.
Novitz, David and Willmott, Bill (ed). *Culture and Identity in New Zealand*, Wellington, 1989.
Oliver, W. H., with Williams, B. R. (ed). *The Oxford History of New Zealand*, Wellington, 1981.
Phillips, Jock. *A Man's Country*, Auckland, 1987.
Reeves, William Pember. *The Long White Cloud*, Auckland, 1950.
Sinclair, Keith (ed). *Tasman Relations*, Auckland, 1987.
Sinclair, Keith. *A History of New Zealand*, London, 1980.

Articles and Report

Arnold, Rollo. 'Some Australasian Aspects of New Zealand Life, 1890-1913', *New Zealand Journal of History*, 4 (1), 1970, 54-76.
Calvert, Ashton. 'The Anzac Link; a Canberra perspective', *New Zealand International Review*, March-April 2001, 6-10.
Downer, Hon. Alexander. 'Australia and New Zealand: a common future in the Asia-Pacific region', *New Zealand International Review*, May-June 2001, 10-13.
Fairburn, Miles. 'New Zealand and Australasian Federation, 1883-1901', *New Zealand Journal of History*, 4 (2), 1970, 138-59.
James, Colin. 'Time to reflect on the A(nz)ac phenomenon', *NZ Herald*, 25 April 2001.
Kirby, Justice Michael. 'The Australia-New Zealand Relationship in the 21st century', *New Zealand Law Journal*, Jan. 1996, 6-7
McLean, Denis. 'Australia and New Zealand: two hearts not beating as one', *New Zealand International Review*, Jan-Feb 2001, 2-6.
Martin, Ged. 'New Zealand, Australian Federation and the "Plain Nonsense" Debate', *British Review of New Zealand Studies*, No. 11, 1998, 67-100.
Rolfe, Mark. 'Faraway Fordism: the Americanization of Australia and New Zealand during the 1950s and 1960s', *New Zealand Journal of History*, 33 (1) 1999, 65-91.
Wood, F.L.W. 'Why did New Zealand not join the Australian Commonwealth in 1900-1901?, *New Zealand Journal of History*, 2 (2), 1968, 115-29.

Australia-New Zealand: Aspects of a Relationship: Proceedings of The Stout Research Centre Eighth Annual Conference, Sept. 1991.

The Cartoonists

Murray Ball is famous for his 'Footrot Flats' cartoon strip and syndicated to 100 newspapers in Australia and New Zealand. Earlier, in Britain, he draw his 'Stanley' and 'Bruce the Barbarian' strips. He co-wrote 'Footrot Flats - the Movie' with Tom Scott, and has published a large number of cartoon collections and other books.

Bob Brockie, with a doctorate in zoology, had a distinguished scientific career, becoming a New Zealand authority on possums and hedgehogs. He has been editorial cartoonist of the weekly *National Business Review* continuously since 1975. He has twice been Qantas cartoonist-of-the-year. He has published several books, two of them cartoon collections.

Peter Bromhead's first cartoons were published in *NZ Truth* and he was then the *Auckland Star's* editorial cartoonist from 1973-89. He now produces page one pocket cartoons for *The Dominion* and a weekly strip for the *Sunday Star Times*. Six times winner of the Qantas cartoonist-of-the-year award, he is a successful interior and furniture designer. He has published several cartoon books.

Chicane (Mark Winter) has been a regular contributor to the *Southland Times* for 25 years and a long-time *PSA Journal* cartoonist. With a masters degree in education, he has been a polytechnic graphics tutor and his film company has won over 20 international awards for its animated shorts and documentary films. He was named Qantas cartoonist-of-the-year in 2000. He served two terms as deputy mayor of Invercargill city.

Malcolm Evans has been cartoonist at the *New Zealand Herald* in Auckland twice, between 1976-78 and since 1994. In between he worked primarily as a commercial artist and developed his enduringly popular rural cartoon characters – Edna and her farmer husband. A number of books of his *Herald* and Edna cartoons have been published. He recently made a TV documentary about his father's wartime experiences.

Eric Heath was a freelance commercial artist before a 1964 invitation to contribute cartoons to the *Dominion Sunday Times* and *The Dominion* led, in 1965, to a 28 year career as the Wellington morning newspaper's political cartoonist. He has published several cartoon collections and illustrated a number of books, particularly in the natural history and maritime fields.

Trace Hodgson contributed political cartoons to the Christchurch *Press* and *New Zealand Times* before becoming the *N.Z. Listener's* political cartoonists for a period from 1984. Today, he contributes cartoons and strips to several publications.

Jim Hubbard, originally a commercial artist, joined the *Daily Telegraph* in Napier as editorial artist and cartoonist in 1985. Now a freelance cartoonist his work appears regularly in *The Dominion, Sunday Star Times, North and South* and other publications.

Ashley Hunter was the *N.Z. Graphic's* cartoonist throughout the 1890s.

Klarc (Laurence Clark) was the *New Zealand Herald's* political cartoonist from 1987-96. He now works from his own Northland studio, primarily pursuing his painting and sculpture interests.

Sir Lionel Lindsay was a prominent Australian painter, graphic artist, writer, and critic. He cartooned, together with his brother Norman, for the Sydney *Bulletin* during the early years of the twentieth century.

The Cartoonists

Trevor Lloyd illustrated stories and articles for the *N.Z. Graphic* before joining the Auckland *Weekly News* in 1903. A pioneer New Zealand etcher, mostly remembered for his studies of native flora and fauna, he drew political cartoons for the *Weekly News* and *New Zealand Herald*, principally the latter between 1910-30.

Nevile Lodge contributed cartoons to army publications during the Second World War. Freelancing after the war, he drew his first 'Lodge Laughs' cartoons for the *Evening Post* in 1947, becoming the Wellington evening daily's political cartoonist in 1956. He freelanced another decade – contributing to the *Free Lance, Truth* and *Listener* – before joining the *Evening Post* staff. He was editorial cartoonist until 1988.

Neil Lonsdale, after a career in advertising, joined the *Auckland Star* as cartoonist in 1952, retiring in 1968. He illustrated a *Women's Weekly* column for another decade.

Sir Gordon Minhinnick was a partly qualified architect in Auckland when the cartooning bug took hold. In the mid-1920s he contributed weekly cartoons to the Wellington-based *Free Lance*, before moving south to become staff cartoonist. His apprenticeship to daily cartooning was six months on the Christchurch *Sun* before joining its newly-launched sister publication, the Auckland *Sun,* in 1927. When this folded in 1930, he joined the *New Zealand Herald*. He officially retired in 1976, but his cartoons appeared regularly for more than another decade. He was knighted in 1976 for his contribution to the cartoonist's craft.

Alan Moir left for overseas after gaining his fine arts degree at Auckland University. He got as far as Australia. Since 1974 he has cartooned for the *Bulletin,* Brisbane *Courier Mail* and, since 1985, as the *Sydney Morning Herald's* political cartoonist. He has been Australian cartoonist-of-the-year six times. His cartoons are syndicated internationally and a number of collections of his cartoons have been published.

Al Nisbet combines editorial cartooning for the Christchurch *Press* with illustration work for its 'Newspapers in Education' supplement. He also provides editorial cartoons to the *Independent*, a weekly business newspaper. He won the Qantas cartoonist-of-the-year award in 1996.

Scatz cartooned for the *N.Z. Graphic* at the beginning of the twentieth century.

Chris Slane, with a town planning degree, has been a freelance cartoonist for most of the last two decades and has created political puppets for television. A three times winner of the Qantas cartoonist-of-the-year award, he has published several books. He is currently the *N.Z. Listener's* cartoonist.

Tom Scott has a physiology graduate from Massey University in Palmerston North where he wrote and cartooned for capping and other campus publications. He was political correspondent for the *N. Z. Listener* for a decade, illustrating his articles with cartoons, then, between 1984-87, wrote and illustrated political columns for the *Auckland Star*, and joined Wellington's *Evening Post* as editorial cartoonist in 1987. He has won the Qantas cartoonist-of-the-year award on five occasions. He has published a number of books, some of them cartoon collections and written TV scripts and made documentary programmes.

Garrick Tremain spent some years in the advertising industry in New Zealand and elsewhere before settling in Queenstown in 1971. A well-established landscape painter, he began political cartooning in 1988 with his work appearing in eight daily newspapers. He has published a number of cartoon collections and has twice been named Qantas cartoonist-of-the-year.

Malcolm Walker has cartooned for a range of publications and has been the *Sunday News's* editorial cartoonist for a number of years. He has published several collections of cartoons and is a two times winner of the Qantas cartoonist-of-the-year award. He is an Auckland architect by day.

The New Zealand Cartoon Archive

The New Zealand Cartoon Archive, launched by then Prime Minister Jim Bolger on 1 April 1992 is the country's national collection of cartoons and caricatures. It is located within the Alexander Turnbull Library in the National Library, Wellington. It is run, in partnership, by the New Zealand Cartoon Archive Trust and the Alexander Turnbull Library which provides a safe, professional, accessible repository fort the Archive. The Trust, with its private sector trustees, raises funds to operate the Archive and support exhibitions and other activities to ensure the widespread promotion of New Zealand cartoons.

The collection includes the work of over 60 New Zealand and expatriate New Zealand cartoonists. Over 20,000 cartoons – originals and copies – have been bequeathed to the Archive by cartoonists and their relatives, collectors, politicians, and organisations. Since 1992, the Archive has received, by arrangement, copies and some originals of the cartoons that appear in the country's newspaper and periodical press. Over 8,700 cartoons have been indexed to date and are available on the Tapuhi internet system http://tapuhi.natlib.govt.nz and 1,045 cartoons and caricatures can be viewed on the National Library's Timeframes http://timeframes.natlib.govt.nz website.

The Cartoon Archive has mounted six exhibitions. Two, featuring famous expatriate cartoonist David Low and rugby football's role in New Zealand life, have toured the country. The others have featured politician Sir Robert Muldoon, cartoonist Eric Heath, the Olympics over five decades, and a selection of year 2000 cartoons. The Cartoon Archive has organised several successful lecture tours and, in June 2001, held New Zealand's first Cartoonists' Convention, attended by most of country's practitioners. In 2001, the Cartoon Archive has assisted L.J. Hooker Ltd establish a national schools' cartooning competition, similar to one the real estate company has been running in Australia for a number of years.

The New Zealand Cartoon Archive can be contacted at P O Box 12349, Wellington, or Tel/Fax: 04 474 3154.

The Author

Ian F. Grant founded the New Zealand Cartoon Archive in 1992, the idea growing out of the research for and writing of *The Unauthorized Version (A Cartoon History of New Zealand)*, and is its executive chairman. A political science and Asian studies graduate of Victoria University, he was creative director of several Wellington advertising agencies before becoming an executive director of *National Business Review* during its first, formative decade and beyond. He was subsequently director of the NZ Book Marketing Council and associate publisher of GP Publications, and has been a director of Auckland communications company, Profile Publishing, for a number of years. He has written or co-authored nine books.

Index

Aboriginals 80, 85
Accents 76, 87
Adams-Schneider, Lance 49
Agents-General 18, 26
Air New Zealand 38, 44
All Blacks 12, 38, 44, 62, 64, 65, 67, 69
America's Cup 68, 71
Anglo-Boer War 29, 48
Ansett 38, 44
Anthony, Doug 49
Anthony, Frank 82
ANZACs 30, 32, 43
ANZAC Pact (also Canberra Pact) 32, 50
ANZAC Ship Project 41
ANZUS Treaty/Alliance 32, 35, 36, 37, 39
Arnold, Rollo 52
Auckland Star 37, 51, 70, 77
Aussie 84

Ball, Murray 81, 84
Balance, John 20
Bank of NZ 55
Beazley, Kim 41
Bledisloe Cup 11, 38
Blomfield, W 25
Bluck, John 80
Bolger, Jim 42
Bond, Alan 68
Britain 10, 14, 16, 18, 20, 22, 24, 29, 30, 31, 32, 34, 50, 62, 64, 78
British Imperial Preference 50
Brockie, Bob 40, 56
Bromhead, Peter 37, 51, 70
Brookes, Norman 62
Bulletin 8, 63

Campion, Jane 86
Canberra Pact (also ANZAC Pact) 32, 50
Catley, Bob 12, 78, 86

Centenary of Federation 11, 13
CER (Closer Economic Relations) 34, 52-3, 59
Chevalier, Nicholas 7
Chicane (Mark Winter) 6, 41, 55
Clark, Helen 13, 43, 58
Clarke, John 84, 86
Clune, Frank 10
Commonwealth Bill 26
Courtenay, Bryce 84
Crowe, Russell 84
Cricket 11, 64, 66, 70, 73, 75, 82

Davis Cup 62
Dominion 33, 39, 71, 79
Douglas, Roger 36, 54, 57
Duffy, Gavan 15

Economic union 12, 38, 52
EEC 34, 50
Eisenhower, Dwight 32
Electric telegraph 18
Evans, Malcolm 49, 87, 89
Evening Post 42, 60, 69, 75

Farming (Australia) 45-6, 48
Farming (New Zealand) 45-8
Fay, Sir Michael 68
Federation (Australia) 10-11, 12, 13, 15, 20, 23, 27
Finey, George 8
'Footrot Flats' 81, 84
Fraser, Malcolm 33

Gallipoli 28, 30, 62, 78, 82
Glover, Tom 8
Goldfields 11, 16, 17, 46
Gore-Browne, Sir Thomas 20
Grimmett, Clarrie 86
GST (Goods and Services Tax) 57

Hall, Sir John 20
Hawke, Bob 35, 40

Hawke's Bay Today 59
Heath, Eric 33, 39, 71, 79
Horse-racing 63
Howard, John 13, 43, 58
Hodgson, Trace 35, 53
Hubbard, Jim 59
Hughes, Billy 8
Humphries, Barry 86
Hunter, Ashley 19, 21, 23, 24, 26

Idress, Ion 84

James, Colin 13
Jokes 80, 82
Joliffe 84

Keating, Paul 11, 42
Kelly, Ned 55
Kenneally, Thomas 12
Klarc (Laurence Clarke) 83
Kiwi 65, 89
Kirby, Justice 13
Korean War 32

Lange, David 35, 36, 37, 40
Lawson, Henry 82
Lee, Dinah 84
Lindsay, Sir Lionel 63
Lloyd, Trevor 65
Lodge, Nevile 67, 69
Lonsdale, Neil 77
Low, Sir David 7-8

Mail services 16, 18
Maori 14, 16, 22, 45, 54, 62, 66, 80
Maritime Strike 21
McCullough, Colleen 84
McLean, Denis 29
Melbourne Age 18
Melbourne Punch 15, 17
Migration 12, 36, 52, 54, 58, 60
Miller, J. D. B. 78
Military settlers 16

Minhinnick, Sir Gordon 31, 47
Moir, Alan 8, 43, 44, 88
Muldoon, Sir Robert 33, 80, 82
Murdoch, Rupert 66

NAFTA (NZ and Australia Free Trade Agreement) 34, 47, 49, 50-3
National Bank of Australia 55
National Business Review 40, 56
Neill, Sam 78
Netball 11, 66
New South Wales 10, 11, 12, 14, 16, 18, 22, 25, 26, 45, 54, 62, 64, 65, 82
N.Z. Graphic 19, 21, 23, 24, 26, 27
N.Z. Herald 31, 47, 49, 76, 83, 87, 89
N.Z. Listener 35, 53, 91
N.Z. Observer 25
Nisbet, Al 52, 73
Northern Territory 81

Olsen, Erik 48
Operation Deep Freeze 77
Otago Daily Times 57, 58, 72, 74, 85

Packer, Kerry 66
Palmer, Nettie 84
Parkes, Sir Henry 13, 20
Paua and the Glory 28
Pavlova 86
Pests 60, 91
Phar Lap 86
Phillips, Jock 64, 78
'Project Blue Sky' 88
PSA Journal 41, 55
Pyke, Vincent 16

Queensland 11, 18, 62, 64, 82

Reagan, Ronald 34, 40
Reeves, William P 22, 26, 45-6
Reid, Sir George 25
Richardson, Ruth 36, 54
Rixon, Steve 73

Rosenburg, Wolfgang 34
Royal Commission on Federation 22, 27
Rugby 11, 62, 64, 65, 66, 67, 69
Rugby League 62, 66, 74

Sargeson, Frank 82
Scott, Tom 12, 28, 42, 60, 75, 84, 91
Scatz 27
Seddon, Richard J. 20, 22, 23, 25
Sheep farming 45-6
Sheep shearers 79, 82
Shute, Nevile 84
Slane, Chris 90
Soccer 60
South Pacific 12, 18, 22, 23, 30, 34, 36, 82
Southland Times 42
Sports Post 67
Sun (Sydney) 8
Sutton, Jim 36-7
Sydney Morning Herald 43, 44, 88

Tasmania 38
Television 66, 68, 88
Tennis 62
Trade 12, 14, 18, 34, 45, 50-2
Tremain, Garrick 57, 58, 72, 74, 85
Trollope, Anthony 78

'Under-arm' incident 59, 66, 70, 73
United States 8, 32, 34, 35, 36, 39, 40, 71, 77
USS Truxton 39

Vietnam War 32, 34
Victoria 12, 15, 16, 17, 19, 45, 62, 82

Walker, Malcolm 6
Ward, Sir Joseph 30
Warne, Shane 75
Wilding, Anthony 62
Wood, F. L. W. 29